The complete guide to
Chinese face
reading

The complete guide to Chinese face reading

JONATHAN DEE

D&S
BOOKS

First published in 2001 by D&S Books

© 2001 D&S Books

D&S Books
Cottage Meadow, Bocombe,
Parkham, Bideford
Devon, England
EX39 5PH

e-mail us at:- enquiries.dspublishing@care4free.net

This edition printed 2001

ISBN 1-903327-20-2

Editorial Director: Sarah King
Editor: Sarah Harris
Project Editor: Yvonne Worth
Designer: Axis Design

Distributed in the UK & Ireland by

Bookmart Limited
Desford Road
Enderby
Leicester LE9 5AD

Distributed in Australia by
Herron Books
39 Commercial Road
Fortitude Valley
Queensland 4006

1 3 5 7 9 10 8 6 4 2

contents

Introduction

Face Reading, or Kang Xiang, is one of the most ancient portions of the considerable mystical traditions of the Chinese. We all like to think that we are experts in 'reading' faces but, as we all know to our cost, this is not generally the case. In fact, most people are actually trying to assess an intention by paying attention to transient facial expressions. It is important to point out that in Kang Xiang it is not facial expression that is being read but the physical features, such as the shape of the face, the size and type of nose, eyes, mouth and ears.

Although the traditional rules of face reading refer to the masculine, oriental face, the same rules can be applied to both sexes and all ethnic types

This ancient art is also still in use in certain aspects of Chinese medicine. However, it is with the oriental traditions of divination and the vagaries of fate that this book is concerned. For many centuries the art of Kang Xiang has been practised and believed throughout China and beyond. Whereas other arts such as palmistry have become familiar, if not accepted, in the western world, face reading has yet to make that leap. Perhaps this book will serve to nudge the process along a little. Throughout the book you will come across various poetic, if sometimes, unflattering, descriptions of face shapes, nose profiles and types of eye. Of course the features these describe must, of necessity, be the average of their type so you may find that a little judicious mixing and matching is required.

It is also a fact that the ancient Chinese had some very sexist attitudes that are not necessarily in tune with current thinking. So, although much of the art of face reading is concerned with masculine features, the rules can, in most cases, be applied to feminine features too. While we are on this subject, throughout this book the pronouns 'he' and 'his' have been applied to the various interpretations of the features. This is for convenience only, avoiding such linguistic awkwardness as 'He or she' and 'his or her', and should not be taken as an expression of sexism on the author's part.

Racial or ethnic type is not important in face reading as, although originally formulated for interpreting Asian facial features, it can be equally effective in interpreting the faces and the features of all ethnic groups.

All that remains to say is enjoy your foray into a little-known oriental discipline. You could discover aspects to the characters of your family and friends that you had never suspected. It may be that there is a side to you that you have attempted to hide only to find that your face is literally an open book.

The symmetry of the features adds to attractiveness and good fortune

Poetic and occasionally unflattering descriptions of eye shapes are part of Kan Xiang

The nose is considered to be the Central Mountain or the Emperor of the face.

Upwardly turning corners of the mouth are considered to be extremely fortunate

The Shape of the Face

People who have learned to draw in the old fashioned way have done so by assuming that the human head resembles an egg upside down. While this may be true from the point of view of classical draughtsmanship, this basic form does allow for certain variations in face shape. Indeed it is by these variations that we recognise friend from foe, the familiar and the strange in those around us. True to form, the ancient Chinese have provided a list of the more usual variations based on their tried and tested philosophy of the five elements.

The Five Elements

Confucius, Lao Tzu and all the other oriental philosophers firmly believed that the universe was in a constant state of change. Lao Tzu in particular once remarked that the only constant in the universe is change. Being a practical people, the Chinese then tried to identify five specific states of being which they expressed in terms that were familiar to them. Each of these states is created by the one preceding it and in turn gives rise to the one that follows. They described these states of being as 'agents of change'. We tend to call them 'elements'. . In

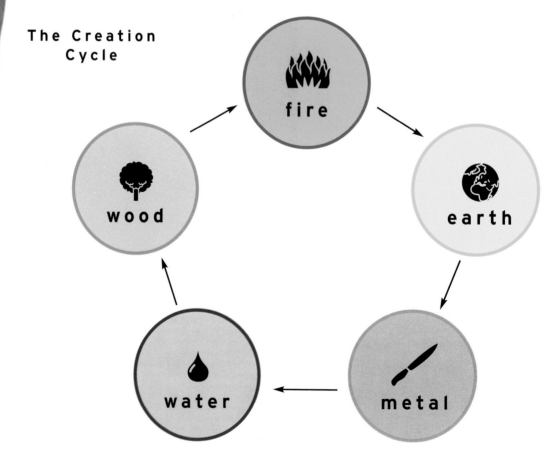

The Creation Cycle

fire

wood

water

earth

metal

Chinese terms these are wood, fire, earth, metal and water and according to ancient symbolism these can be arranged into a circular form known as 'The Creation Cycle', a concept that will be familiar to anyone who takes an interest in Feng Shui. According to this cycle wood is burned to feed fire, fire creates earth in the form of ash, the depths of the earth give birth to metal which, when molten, flows like water, water in turn feeds the growth of wood.

However, this system has a down side because, should the sequence be disrupted, chaos and destruction can occur. Beginning again with wood, wood exhausts earth, earth fouls water, water quenches fire, fire melts metal, metal chops wood. This of course is the Cycle of Destruction.

Apart from the obvious qualities of the elements, the philosophers of old also attributed other characteristics to them such as particular compass directions, colours, animals, plants and, most vital to face reading, character definitions and individual geometric shapes. Thus the element wood was symbolised by the rectangle, fire by the triangle, earth by the square, metal by the oval and water by the circle. So there are five basic face shapes, each of which has an association with one of the agents of change. In addition to these there are also two variations that are recognised but do not strictly fit within the elemental system. These are 'the Volcano Face' which is a Fire type variant and 'the Bucket Face' which is of the Metal type.

Symbol	Element
🌳	WOOD
🔥	FIRE
🌍	EARTH
🔪	METAL
💧	WATER

The Destruction Cycle

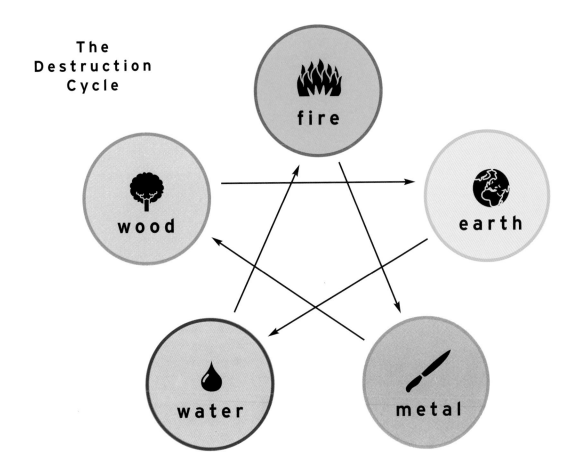

The Wood Face

The wood type of face is rectangular in appearance. It has a uniformity of width and is far longer than it is wide. The forehead of this type of face is likewise high and usually possesses well-defined creases. In men there is often a receding hairline. The general aspect of this face is both genial and dignified. This is a face type associated with warmth and optimism. The possessor of the Wood Face is energetic, with leadership potential, strong ideals and determination. He is popular, wins friends easily and is charitable. He will stand up for a point of principle and have a philosophical attitude towards life. Although the owner of the Wood Face is kindly and benevolent he can also demand that things are done his way and he may occasionally express himself in an arrogant manner because, although he means well, he can be pretty tactless in imposing his views. The Wood Face is also associated with strong religious or philosophical convictions. However, care must be taken that the sense of always being right does not turn a positive and uplifting viewpoint into harmful fanaticism.

The Fire Face

The fiery type of face is recognised by a wide jaw and a narrow forehead. In shape therefore it resembles an upward pointing triangle, the shape symbolic of fire. It is said that the gaze of someone with a Fire Face can be quite daunting because the angry look in the eyes can cow all but the bravest. As might be imagined, the temperament of a person with a Fire Face is likely to be rather heated and excitable resulting from an unhappy childhood or other factors of a distressing background. The ambitions of this type are also very strong since he has a desire to remove himself as far from his origins as possible. This desire also provides a key to his lack of patience and outbursts of anger when his plans are thwarted. On the other hand, fire faced people tend to be lucky, highly sexed, physically attractive and can be extremely persuasive and charming. However his boiling point is very low and he can show an altogether less pleasant face when he loses his self-control. Of course, extremes of this type can be violent, and even the most relatively mild mannered Fire-faced person usually has a string of broken relationships in his past.

The Earth Face

This type of face is noticeably square, its height and width being apparently the same. The complexion tends to be ruddy, the hair often bushy and the eyes, somewhat red but expressive of authority. The nose and mouth also will tend to be wide, however the lips are usually quite thin and the teeth small. The Earth Face is an indicator of toughness and determination, although some would claim that it is more likely to be utterly stubborn. The energy levels are high and there is a tendency to immediately leap to conclusions before the facts are fully known. A person with an Earth Face is used to other people walking on eggshells around him because his temper is quick and unpredictable. However, other people are rarely the problem since this type of person can impulsively get himself into trouble with no help from anyone else. Those around him then become his saviours because, although he can get himself into it, he lacks the inner strength to extricate himself without considerable help. A person with this type of face enjoys good health, has an active social life and may at some time become involved in contact sports such as American Football, or Rugby.

The Metal Face

The Metal Face is the opposite of the Fire types. It is rather oval but can be thought of as an inverted triangle, widest at the top, working its way down to a pointed chin. The facial features are regular and rather refined, however the mouth may either be slightly too large or small. The fairly large eyes are lively and active denoting intelligence and sharp perceptions. The possessor of this type of face lives in his head. He would consider himself to be far more of an intellectual than a manual worker but might actually prefer it if he were not. His mind is extremely active and rarely gives him any peace. He has difficulty in relaxing and may have been quite a handful when he was a child. He loves talking and is not averse to a heated debate as long as he is sure of his ground. However, even when he isn't he is quite capable of turning the tables on his opponent with clever word play and a dazzling display of wit. Although he likes meeting new people he will keep all but a few at a distance because emotional closeness is disturbing to him. A person with a Metal-type face is a born politician, a salesman and organiser. He is likely to be ambitious and can be quite cunning.

The Water Face

The Water Face is easy to recognise because it is round, and in the west we tend to call this type 'the Moon Face'. This sort of face is traditionally said to be pale or drained of colour – often indicative of poor circulation. The eyes, in common with the ruling element, are said to be watery. People with Water Faces are often accused of being lazy but this is not the case. It is true that they tend to lack energy and often become tired and lethargic, but that is not quite the same thing. The one thing that Water-faced people have an abundance of is imagination. They have a rich and rare fantasy world

that is often a more comfortable place to inhabit than the real one. On the other hand, this vivid imagination can give rise to unrealistic expectations, disappointments, and possibly hypochondria. People with Water Faces are also quite dependent on others for reassurance and support. Lacking in self-confidence they will cling to those around them for comfort. If they find themselves alone for any length of time they will tend to prevaricate, putting off decisions for as long as possible.

The Volcano Face

This is a variant of the true Fire Face but is far more common. The Volcano is also triangular in general outline but more generally resembles a truncated pyramid, flattening at the forehead. This type of face is also rather bony with a lack of facial softness about it. It is also quite sallow in complexion and often is identifiable by the number of moles that are present. Like the true Fire Face the Volcano type probably did not have a very happy childhood. There is an inner anger or resentment bubbling beneath the surface and this can provide a spur to make great improvements, develop big ambitions and generally to deal with the world on his own terms. However there is more self-control than the fire type and annoyance is more likely to be expressed through bitter words and sarcasm than through outbursts of anger. This self-control gives another clue to this character because he is fairly solitary by preference and may have unusual ideas and enthusiasms. Deep and thoughtful, he nevertheless can deal with others as long as they do not cross him, and is possessed of a high sex drive.

The Bucket Face

This is a variant on the Metal-type of face. In this case the shape is the opposite of the 'Volcano Face', a truncated triangle that is widest at the top descending to a flattened chin. Possessors of the Bucket Face are artistic because it in some ways combines the hard determination of metal with the softer qualities of water. This type is intelligent, perceptive, witty, and quick on the uptake and can have many varied interests. However, the cunning and coolness of the true metal-type is not so evident here. A person with a Bucket Face may be easily hurt, can be overly sensitive and very aware of another's pain. This is an outgoing personality who loves to be loved, and needs the approval of those around him. This could be difficult because he wants to enjoy himself with many different types of people from all walks of life and, as we all know, it's hard to please all of the people all of the time. Hard lessons are usually learned this way because there are many who are all too willing to take advantage of this person's goodwill. It is not uncommon for the owner of the Bucket Face to marry young for reasons of security.

The Divisions of the Face

The oriental face readers of old have left us with a bewildering amount of information categorising the face into various sections for the purposes of divination. In fact, we now have 130 distinct positions of the features that possess individual significance.

The Three Regions of the Face

Fortunately, we don't have to worry too much about all 130 positions, but shall concentrate instead on the Three Regions of the face that divide the features into vertical areas. The Heavenly or Celestial Region occupies the area from the hairline to the eyebrows. The Human Region or Region of Self-will extends from the eyebrows to the tip of the nose. Finally the Earthly Region covers the area from the nose tip to the point of the chin. In terms of age projections these three regions represent youth, middle and old age in that order.

The Heavenly Region

The Heavenly or Celestial Region corresponds to the brow. If the brow is clear, even and smooth this means good fortune and a happy, supportive family in early life. However, should this area be lumpy with a dull, greyish complexion it can suggest an unsettled childhood. A wide forehead is considered to be a good omen, but if it is too wide then romantic life especially will be subject to unsettling influences (see The Brow pp.61-73).

The Human Region

The Human Region or Region of Self-will comprises that area of the face that is home to the nose and the cheekbones. In terms of age this area corresponds to the middle years. In general, the more regular the features here the more settled and stable the person will be. Any disproportionate feature will have an unfortunate effect, especially in terms of marital or other close emotional relationships during this period. If the Human Region happens to be longer than either of the other two regions then the person's ability to take control of life and bend it to his will is very evident. If the complexion here is dull and greyish then there will be many career upheavals in middle age (see The Nose and Cheekbones pp.85-96).

The Earthly Region

A good bone structure is the first consideration when considering the Earthly area. Proportion and a good balance of features are important factors in determining whether the subject will have a happy, healthy and fulfilling old age or not. The mouth too falls within this region, and examination of the shape and thickness of the lips is also a good indicator of one's fate. Thin lips combined with a narrow or receding chin are signs of a weak constitution (See The Lips and Mouth pp.104-113 and The Chin and Jaw pp.119-125).

The Five Predominant Features

It almost goes without saying that the five predominant features of the face are the eyes, the eyebrows, the mouth, the nose and the ears. If these features are in proportion to each other then a life filled with good fortune, prosperity, happiness and health is foretold. However, should one of them be 'out of place' or disproportionately small or large this will seriously detract from a person's luck. A bent or broken nose, an inward turned eye, a twisted lip or a scarred eyebrow all serve to indicate an area of discord in a subject's life. On the other hand, if any of these features are absolutely perfectly formed then fate will take a hand to improve matters even in the darkest hours.

The three significant zones
of the face

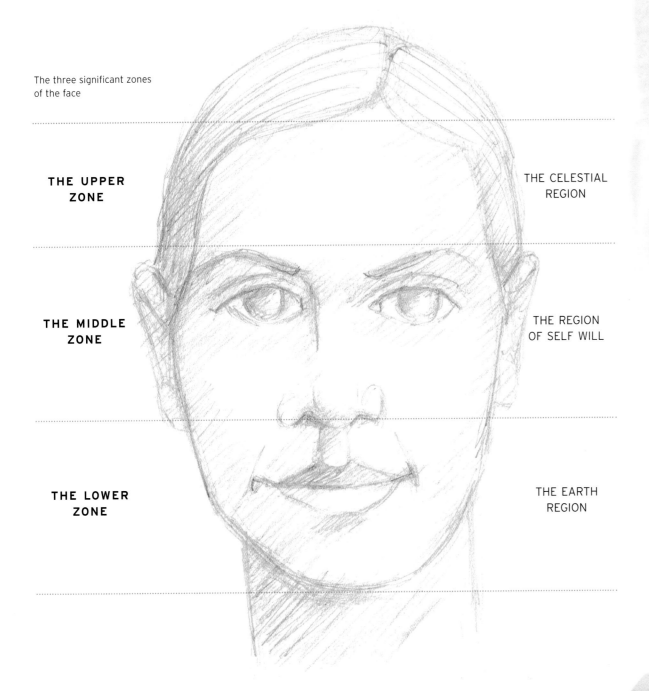

**THE UPPER
ZONE**

THE CELESTIAL
REGION

**THE MIDDLE
ZONE**

THE REGION
OF SELF WILL

**THE LOWER
ZONE**

THE EARTH
REGION

The Age Positions of the Face

The ancient sages have also provided us with facial age positions, which are dotted about the face and ears highlighting particular years in a person's life. The most important of these are known as the Thirteen Significant Positions. These points are found running in a straight line from the hairline to the tip of the chin. The Significant Positions deal with the subject's life from the ages of fifteen to seventy one.

The Thirteen Significant Positions

1 T'ien Chung

The T'ien Chung or 'Middle Heaven' is the highest position of the Heavenly Region and is found just below the mid-point of the hairline. This position is particularly relevant to the fifteenth year of life. If you do not find a scar, blemish or mole here it is a sign of a happy childhood and consequently of a strong affection with the parents. If greyish or black marks are found on the T'ien Chung then early poverty and an unhappy youth are revealed. If a vein or other strong line is present running into the hairline it indicates the risk of accidents or failure when success seems certain.

The age positions of the face

2 T'ien T'ing

This area is particularly related to the eighteenth year. The skin tone of this position is considered to be especially important. If the skin is clear and free of blemishes with a healthy colour then it is said to be a good indication of a strong parental bond. Influential friends will have a positive effect throughout life and help will be readily given when the subject most needs it. However, should the skin here have a grey tinge it is a sign that the person will be unable to convince others of the truth. If such a mark, called a 'black cloud', suddenly appears it is an omen of grave misfortune that will occur within two weeks.

3 Ssu K'ung

The colour of this section of the Heavenly Region is the determining factor of fortune and is relevant to age twenty-one. If the Ssu K'ung has a red or yellow tinge it is a good omen indicating the respect of others and good advice. However should the area be grey or black there will be short periods of bad luck. As with T'ien T'ing, the sudden appearance of a grey mark warns of swift misfortune, in this case in the working life.

4 Chung Cheng

This particularly refers to age twenty-four and the area should be clear and without blemish. If this is so then good fortune and early successes will be attained. If the skin surface is dented or uneven then the subject will lack concentration. A black mole here severely reduces the patience and the person may constantly find himself in the wrong place at the wrong time.

5 Yin T'ang

Good clear skin with a healthy colour foretells a large inheritance and shrewdness in business. However, should the gap between the eyebrows be too narrow there will be financial misfortunes, especially around the twenty-seventh year. If the eyebrows meet in the middle of the Yin T'ang then this is a person who cannot always be trusted to tell the truth or to act honourably. A scar or birthmark in this area is said to signify adoption. A black mole in the Yin T'ang can reveal long-term illnesses while a mole to one side of this area foretells legal problems (see also Vertical Creases p.68)

6 Shan Ken

This is the meeting point between the Heavenly and the Human Regions of the face. It relates to the fortieth year of life. This area should have a pronounced yet gentle dip to provide harmony between the influences of fate and mortal actions. If a dark patch of skin is found in this area a short period of illness is foretold. The darker the area the longer the illness will last. A mole here reveals a move away from home to find work. A mole on one side of the Shan Ken shows that the subject is prone to stomach ailments.

7 Nien Shang

The Nien Shang is that area of the nose at the end of the nasal bone and is most associated with the emotions and the physical constitution as well as the forty-third year. A mole here can show a troubled romantic life as well as highlighting stomach disorders even though the general state of health is good (see also The Nose and Cheekbones pp.85-96).

8 Shou Shang

The Shou Shang is found mid-way between the Nien Shang and the tip of the nose and relates to the forty-fourth year. A lump found here is a bad omen suggesting failed business enterprises. It is also grim news for the romantic life. However, if the skin on both sides of this point is good and clear then there will be a stylish fashion sense and a strong constitution (see also The Nose and Cheekbones pp.85-96).

9 Chun T'ou

The Chun T'ou at the tip of the nose is a very important area. Take special notice of the pores here because if they are enlarged or have dark hairs growing from them it is likely to be a sign of poverty especially around age forty-seven.

10 Jen Chung

This area is also called the philtrum. It corresponds to the fiftieth year of life and is so important that it has a section devoted to it on pp.114-118.

11 Shui Hsing

This is the area of the lips relating to age fifty-nine and has been dealt with in its own section on pp.104-113.

12 Ch'eng Chiang

This sector refers to age sixty-nine and is the beginning of the chin area, a sector of the face governed by the water element. It therefore has connections with both the imbibing of liquids and with travels by water. Tradition states that if a dark patch appears here you should reduce your intake of liquids and postpone voyages until it vanishes. Very pale, greenish or dark red patches signify poisoning or at least an infection taken in via drink.

13 Ti Ko

The tip of the chin, relating to age seventy is fully dealt with in The Chin and Jaw pp.119-125.

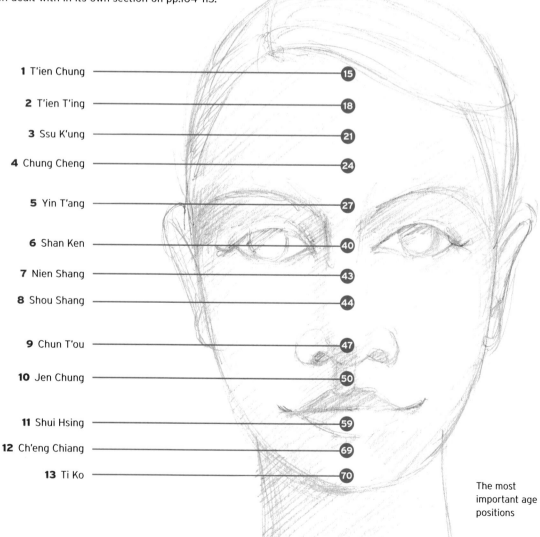

1 T'ien Chung — 15
2 T'ien T'ing — 18
3 Ssu K'ung — 21
4 Chung Cheng — 24
5 Yin T'ang — 27
6 Shan Ken — 40
7 Nien Shang — 43
8 Shou Shang — 44
9 Chun T'ou — 47
10 Jen Chung — 50
11 Shui Hsing — 59
12 Ch'eng Chiang — 69
13 Ti Ko — 70

The most important age positions

The Twelve Earthly Stems

Ages above the seventy-first year are dealt with by the Twelve Earthly Stems which are found around the circumference of the face and deal with ages ranging from seventy one to one hundred. We in the west may be more familiar with the Stems in their guise as the twelve animal signs of the Chinese Zodiac. These are Rat, Ox, Tiger, Rabbit, Dragon, Snake, Horse, Goat, Monkey, Rooster, Dog and Pig. No specific interpretations are given for the Stems but some facts can be gleaned from the colour, texture and general condition of the skin in these areas.

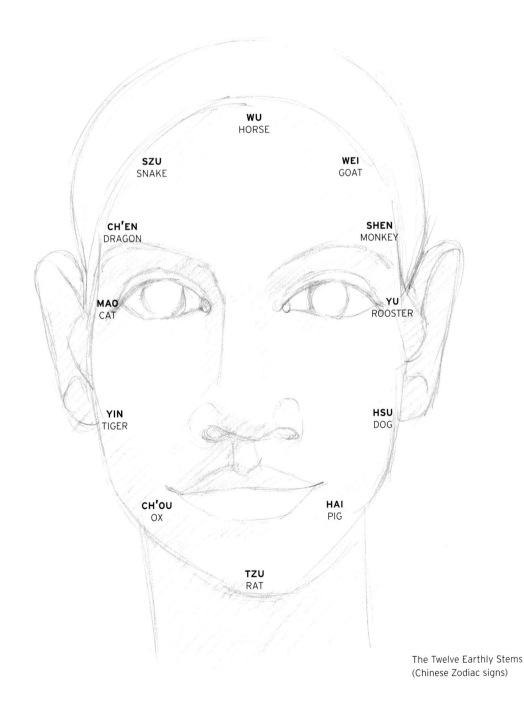

The Twelve Earthly Stems
(Chinese Zodiac signs)

The Twelve Palaces of Fortune

Apart from the readings concerning the various age positions there are also areas that are roughly analogous to the astrological houses of a horoscope chart. In Chinese terms these are called the Palaces of Fortune. Like the divisions of the horoscope chart these Palaces deal with specific topics such as home, material wealth, career, love, destiny and so on. Some of these Palaces occur in two places – at each temple, above and below the eye and so on – others have only one location.

The Twelve Palaces

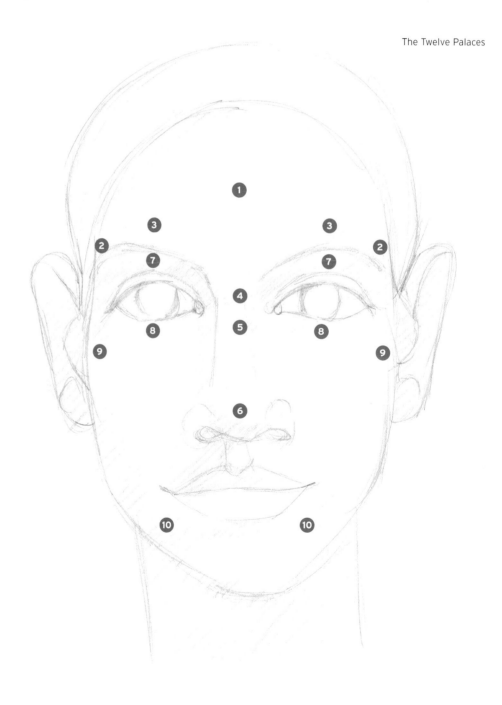

1 Kaun Lu Kung

The Palace of Career - This area lies in the centre of the brow and should be clear and unblemished. Lasting friendships and influential help is indicated when this area is perfectly formed. However, if the area is too prominent or too sunken it indicates hard times and great obstacles placed in the path of achieving career goals. A mole here shows a need to persevere to achieve one's ambitions.

2 Ch'ien I Kung

The Palace of Movement - There are actually two palaces of Movement - one on each temple. If this area is hollow with no protruding bones or lumps, successful journeys are to be expected. In fact, should the skin on this area be completely clear, this person is likely to be an inveterate traveller or intrepid explorer. The sudden appearance of dark patches here warns that planned journeys should be put off. A mole here shows the possibility of theft or loss of possessions through accidents when travelling.

3 Hsiung Ti Kung

The Palace of Brothers - The areas directly above the eyebrows are called the Palace of Brothers and refer not only to those who are blood relations but also to those who become one's brothers (and indeed sisters) throughout life. In practice this Palace is dependent on the shape and length of the eyebrows themselves. Long well-formed eyebrows denote happy relationships, broken or scarred eyebrows mean the opposite (see The Eyebrows pp.47-60).

4 Min Kung

The Palace of Life - This area is most concerned with the state of the emotions. It is found between the eyebrows in the area known as Shan Ken. If this area is wrinkled then there will be troubling affairs of the heart, but if this position is clear then happy relationships and a fortunate emotional life are forecast. However, the total absence of wrinkles after the age of thirty is the sign of a daydreamer and time waster (see Shan Ken p.19)

5 Chi O Kung

The Palace of Sickness – Although the name of this palace is rather negative it does govern the general state of one's health. It is found at the bridge of the nose around the area of the Nien Shang. Good nose shape, clear complexion and an absence of blemishes are good signs for the constitution. However, should this area be criss-crossed by small lines or marked with a scar or a mole then many minor illnesses are foretold (see also Nien Shang p.19 and The Nose and Cheekbones pp.85–96).

6 Ts'ai Pai Kung

The Palace of Wealth – As the name implies, material well-being is revealed by examination of this palace, which lies at the tip of the nose. Indeed the shape of this area is of the first importance when it comes to assessing the possibilities of making and retaining wealth (see Chun T'ou p.19 and The Nose and Cheekbones pp.85–96). Apart from the purely financial aspect of this area it also has a bearing on personal attitudes and a readiness to take responsibility for one's own actions. If a natural blemish is found on the nose tip it may show a person who is too ready to accept blame and carries the weight of the world on his shoulders. A scar here warns of danger both to one's health and relationships in the forty-fourth year of life.

7 T'ien Chai Kung

The Palace of House and Farm – This palace governs domestic life and the fortunes of the family and livestock, pets etc. It is found in two areas just above each eye. As usual, if these areas are clear and of healthy colour the outlook is good, but if one or other is scarred, blemished or very grey, peace of mind will be hard to achieve. A mole in either area is an indication that part of the subject's life will be lived in poverty and squalor.

8 Nan Nu Kung

The Palace of Man and Woman – This is another area concerned with family relationships. It is found in two areas, both being immediately under the eyes. Of course the eye shape and the conditions of the surrounding skin is important to this sector (see The Eyes pp.29–46). However should these palaces be very lumpy, baggy, overly wrinkled or very grey then one's family will be a source of continuous worry. If the lines here cross over each other then leaving home early in life is a distinct possibility. Criss-crossed lines here are also an indication of strained family relationships and it is unlikely that the subject will keep in regular contact with his parents.

11 Fu Te Kung

The Palace of Fortune and Virtue - There is no single area allocated to the Palace of Fortune and Wealth. In fact the very name of the palace is a euphemism for facial expressions that are revealing of mental processes and emotional states. Thus, a smile signifying happiness would be considered an aspect of the Palace of Fortune and Wealth. The interpretation of these transient signs is the only time when expressions enter the realm of Chinese Face Reading.

9 Ch'I Ch'ien Kung

The Palace of the Wife and Mistress - This palace, which is found in two areas corresponding to the cheekbones, seeks to ascertain the character of the partner in life. In the case of men, this reading is usually taken from the left-hand cheek, for women it is taken on the right. In practice, as long as the cheekbones do not protrude too much the significant other will be a good judge of character and a reliable and virtuous person. If the skin is very tight here then marital relations will become strained. If there is a dent here then infidelity can be expected. A mole in either Ch'I Ch'ien indicates a flirtatious and wicked spouse.

12 Hsiang Mao Kung

The Palace of the Face - Like the 11th Palace, the Palace of the Face has no single area allocated to it. In fact, this palace is the summation of face reading and its interpretation is the subject of this book. In short the Palace of the Face is the art of Kang Xiang.

10 Nu P'u Kung

The Palace of Servants - The two areas that comprise the Palace of Servants are found on either side of the chin. These areas not only describe the attitudes of and relationships to one's subordinates, but also the state of more equal friendships. If these two areas have a good, well-rounded shape friends and subordinates will tend to be trustworthy people who will rely on the subject's judgements. However should the area be wrinkled, blemished or lack tone then the subject will make unnecessary enemies and be notorious for tactlessness.

The Five Mountains

As has been previously stated, the Chinese regard the face as a landscape with physical features that are akin to a map of the earth. Thus the face has five mountains, each of which have been given symbolic names.

Those who are familiar with the equally ancient art of Feng Shui will instantly recognise these symbolic forms as being identical to those employed for the five directional forces that form the basis of this other mystical discipline. In Feng Shui terms the Red Bird symbolises the south and the fire element. The Green Dragon represents the east and the element wood, the Yellow Emperor stands for earth at the centre while the White Tiger and the Black Tortoise occupy the west and the north respectively being symbolic of the elements metal and water.

The Right Cheek
The Mountain of the White Tiger

The Brow
The Mountain of the Red Bird

The Left Cheek
The Mountain of the Green Dragon

The Chin
The Mountain of the Black Tortoise

The five mountains

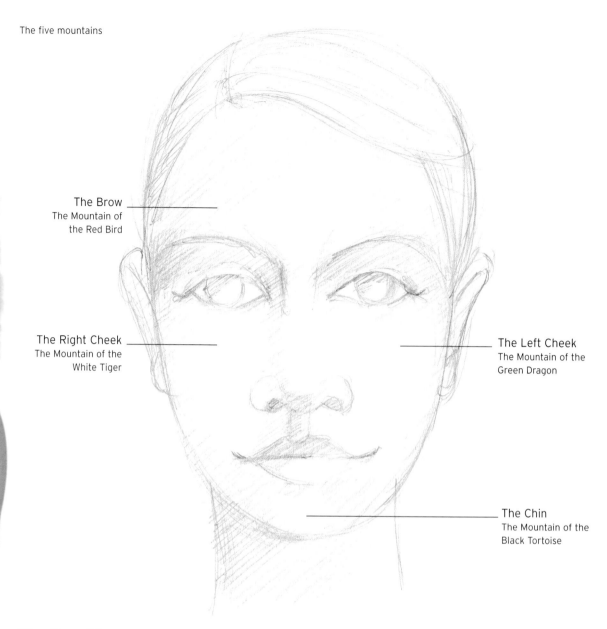

The Brow
The Mountain of
the Red Bird

The Right Cheek
The Mountain of the
White Tiger

The Left Cheek
The Mountain of the
Green Dragon

The Chin
The Mountain of the
Black Tortoise

The Four Rivers

Apart from the mountains of the facial landscape the ancient masters also recognised four rivers.

The River Kong – The Ears
The River Ho – The Eyes
The River Wai – The Mouth
The River Chai – The Nostrils

Tradition states that the waters of these rivers should be clear and clean. This not only refers to the liquids that are found in these areas but also to the flow of the chi or life-force which both enters and is expelled from these regions of the face. The ancient Chinese considered chi to have two forms, sheng chi, which is positive and life giving, and sha chi, which is dark and unwholesome. To put it simply chi arrives in the ears in its positive form as sound and the dark or stagnant chi leaves in the form of wax. The chi entering the eyes does so in the form of light and leaves in the form of tears. Likewise breath is the sheng chi of the nostrils while mucus is the sha chi. It is only the mouth that can take in and expel chi in both of its forms as good food or bad, kind words or harsh ones.

THE EYES

In western culture the eyes are said to be the windows of the soul, and that is very much the case in Chinese face reading. The eyes are the single most important feature of the face and are considered to 'control' all the other characteristics including the nose, which is otherwise described as the emperor of the face. When practising this ancient art the interpretation of the appearance and areas around the eyes is the usual starting point. This is because the eyes alone remain the same throughout life whereas the nose, ears, hairline and mouth are subject to change through growth and ageing.

In the age position chart of face reading, the eyes signify the mid to late thirties. The inner whites of the eyes relate to 34 on the right and 35 on the left. The right pupil correlates to 36 while the left relates to age 37. The outer whites represent 38 on the right and 39 on the left.

The Colours of the Eye

It may seem surprising to westerners, but eye colour is not considered to be an important factor in the interpretation of this area of the face. This is because this form of face reading developed in China and among oriental peoples an iris of dark brown to black hue is usual. Whatever colour the iris happens to be, its tone should be distinct and not flecked with another hue.

On the other hand, a system of classification of eye colour has been developed in the west due to the variety of eye colours present in the Caucasian races. Hazel eyes denote emotional warmth and a keen intellect. People with ordinary brown eyes are said to be extroverted and excitable but also conservative and cautious deep down. It is also claimed that they are less sensitive to pain than those with lighter shades.

Blue eyes can vary greatly in hue from deep sapphire to a pale watery grey-blue. The general rule here is the greater the depth of colour the greater the passion. People with blue eyes are said to be quieter, more calm and compassionate than their brown-eyed compatriots. Those with very pale eyes can be extremely cool and calculating while those with a darker blue are more

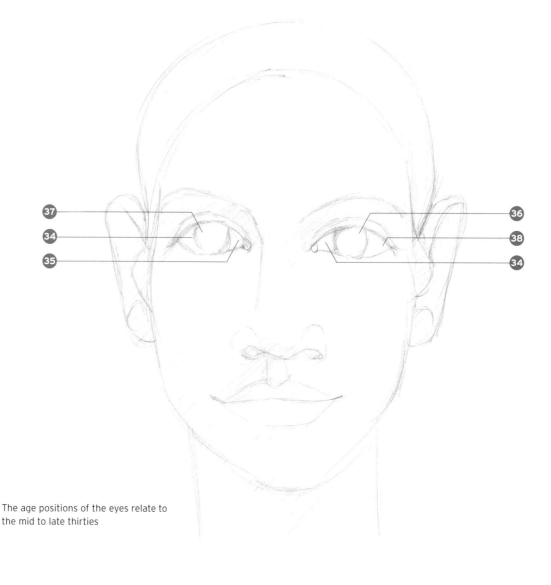

The age positions of the eyes relate to
the mid to late thirties

passive and like a quiet life. Those with truly grey eyes, are quite rare, and the colour denotes someone who is logical, emotionally controlled and possibly vacillating. This type needs to consider any matter in great depth before committing himself to any course of action.

People with green eyes are claimed to be daring individuals with inventive thought processes and a cheerful personality.

Of course, none of the above applies to people who are not of European ancestry so the significance of eye colour to Chinese Face Reading remains in doubt.

General Characteristics

The eye is interpreted according to its overall shape, clarity and position. The 'perfect eye' should have a large iris, but not so large that it almost completely covers the whites. However, too small an iris suggests a person who is accident-prone, one who may not seek trouble, but nevertheless constantly encounters it in one form or another (see 'The Four White Eye' p.36).

In general terms, eyes should not be bloodshot or have prominent and visible blood vessels. In short, the brighter the pupil, the better. In addition, the eyes should not bulge out too much or habitually look angry.

Someone who holds your eye when talking with you is most likely to be trustworthy

Big, wide eyes indicate a friendly, but shrewd, person

If the eyes of the person you are considering are somewhat dull, or the most notable feature is a pair of low, heavy eyebrows this is compared to thick clouds obscuring the light of the moon. Such a configuration is indicative of a person who is a great planner but concerns himself with too much detail. Such a person is one who rarely puts his schemes into action. It may also indicate someone who promises a great deal but rarely delivers.

Big, wide eyes are an indicator that the person is friendly, happy-go-lucky in private life but quite shrewd and has a keen business sense.

Dark, deep eyes show that there is an active mind at work and hints at a nature that is artistic and talented. Very round staring eyes or eyes that protrude are indicative of someone who is a hard worker but has known great misfortune. Events rarely turn out well for this individual and he must make enormous efforts to ensure that all his plans do not go completely awry.

Someone who can hold your eye with his own is likely to be reliable and honest. He is reasonable and forthright, willing to accept the opinions of others and is unlikely to be overly stubborn.

A person whose eyes look you up and down while you are speaking is a careful calculator. Shrewd and possibly scheming, this person is very practical but cannot be totally relied upon.

Watery eyes, which are nevertheless well-shaped and adequately spaced, indicate a powerfully sexual nature. People with this characteristic are bound to be wicked flirts.

A person who raises his eyes while speaking is extremely confident in his opinions. This person is rarely afraid to voice his opinions and will stick to his views through thick and thin... whether they are correct or not.

Quick, darting eyes denote a person with numerous

Upwardly sloping crow's feet signify happiness in relationships and luck

The Slope of the Eye

The inclination or slope of the eye is also important. Ideally the eyes should lie along a horizontal plane, although it is possible that they will noticeably incline upwards or downwards. If there is an upward slope their possessor will be an extremely proud and wilful individual. This is the mark of an extrovert who has great confidence and is capable of making the most of all the opportunities that come his way.

The opposite is the case when the eyes slope downwards, giving the face a rather sad or mournful aspect. Nevertheless this individual is quite cheerful even though he is rather introverted. This type is extremely sympathetic and is usually a sucker for a sob story. He is an enabler, ensuring that those around him make the most out of their potentials. Caring, charitable and kind, this personality is likely to enjoy a long and happy emotional relationship.

Crow's Feet

Four or less narrow wrinkles at the edge of the eye can be a general indicator of the course of luck throughout life. If the person is over forty years of age the appearance of small wrinkles or 'crow's feet' around the eyes (especially at the outside edge) is a normal indicator of ageing. If, however the person is youthful, then the appearance of crow's feet takes on an extra significance. Their presence will suggest remarkable organisational abilities as well as a tendency to revel in challenges. This type of person is one to have on your side in difficult situations. If the wrinkles incline upwards this is considered to be a very auspicious sign signifying good fortune and happiness in relationships. However, if the wrinkles incline downwards work difficulties and financial problems are indicated. Relationship harmony may also be difficult to achieve. The picture is even worse when the 'crow's feet' have a scissor-like appearance, crossing over each other in opposite directions so that some go upwards and some downwards. This shows a personality who finds it difficult to accept advice or admit to his mistakes. Family tensions and emotional turmoil are a strong possibility. It is also likely to reveal someone who is only truly happy when he is complaining about something.

Very long 'crow's feet' reveal a lustful nature and problems with commitment. Divorce is a fairly common occurrence in the lives of these people, who are also likely to have a series of unsatisfactory relationships. The extra long wrinkles may also suggest that this is a person who is something of a sponger - loving money but unwilling to work for it.

Although four wrinkles at the outer edge of the eye is normal, the existence of many lines can be regarded as a sign of personal isolation and can point to loneliness. If this occurs in someone who is young, the crow's feet suggest laziness and lack of purpose.

According to the age positions of the face, the area of crow's feet at the outer edge of the eye relate to the 28th year on the right and the 29th on the left.

Crossed or 'scissor-like' crow's feet signify a difficulty in admitting mistakes or accepting advice

Downward sloping crow's feet
indicate career problems and
financial difficulties

The Upper Eyelids

A fold upon the upper eyelid shows great self-control. If no fold is present then overwhelming reactions to emotional dramas is likely.

It has also been noted that untrustworthy people tend to possess eyelids that droop down in the centre giving the face a rather sleepy appearance. This is often known as 'bedroom eyes' and, as the name implies, suggest a preoccupation with seduction. In Chinese tradition such an eyelid denotes someone who is cunning, self-serving and without conscience.

The Lower Eyelids

Should the lower eyelid droop to reveal the red inner surface then the conclusions drawn from this tend to be sexual in nature. In a woman it is said that her character is likely to be lustful and wanton while in a man, that he is likely to be impotent.

Determination is shown
by the Three White Eye

The Traditional Types of Eye

Chinese tradition holds that there are many different types of eye shape dependent on the surrounding features of the eyeball and the position of the iris itself. In keeping with most other aspects of oriental culture these shapes have been given suitably poetic (if sometimes unflattering) names relating to their interpretation.

The Three White Eye

This type has the iris at the bottom of the eye with the white to the left, right and above. It is said to denote a personality that is determined and extremely confident. This is so much so that the capacity for wilfulness leads to outbursts of foul temper. This is a person who is too easily frustrated by the slow actions and apparent inefficiency of others. On the plus side, the possessor of the Three White Eye is totally truthful, although, it must be said, somewhat forthright and often tactless.

The Wolf's Eye

The opposite of the Three White Eye, the Wolf's Eye describes the iris floating just under the upper eyelid, the white to the left, right and below. This type of person is very shrewd. They are rarely at a loss and generally know exactly what they want. What is more, the possessor of this type of eye is astute enough to get it. Traditionally, people with eyes of this type are said to have a capacity for cruelty or at least to act without consideration to the feelings of others. People with Wolf's Eyes are no strangers to conflict and will encounter opposition throughout life. It is this factor that defines their ruthless determination.

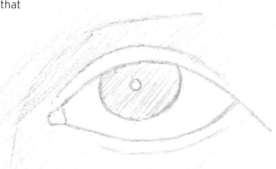

The Wolf's Eye

The Four White Eye

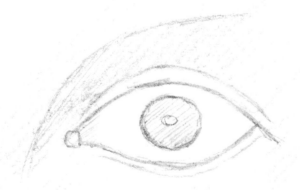

The Four White Eye

This type of eye has the iris set in the very middle of the eyeball. The white surrounds it on all sides and it is often associated with eyes that are prominent or bulge. Possessors of this type of eye are used to being surprised, and are quite adept at handling the most unexpected situations. However this adaptability turns to outbursts of fury when cherished personal plans are thwarted by the dictates of fate. This type of person is very good at anticipating events and working out alternative schemes. It is only when their personal 'plan B' goes awry do they tend to lose their cool.

The Triangular Eye

The upper eyelid has a distinct raised portion in the middle. The colour of the iris tends to be strong, and its surrounding tends to be somewhat off-white. This type of eye is normally associated with a strong eyebrow. The Triangular Eye is said to be a sure sign of great success in life. People who possess this feature will be competitive and always up for a challenge. Great observers of life, they nevertheless know when to be passive and when to act. A true politician - although some would say plotter. The Triangular Eye person will make the most out of the opportunities presented to him and achieve wealth and status as a result. Although this type is generally benevolent there is a streak of ruthlessness and literally an eye for the main chance.

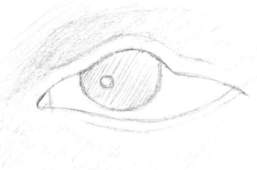

The Triangular Eye

The Angry Eye

The Angry Eye is notable for concentric circles within the iris. This type of eye is also known as the Wheel Eye. This type of configuration describes someone who is noted more for his physical presence than his mental acuteness, less of a thinker and more of a doer. However there is a marked determination in this type even though the consequences of actions are rarely well thought out. Even so this person's desires are usually accomplished even if they bring chaos in their wake. It is the defence of such actions that gives rise to the description of this type as the Angry Eye. In truth, the possessor of this type of eye is rarely aware of what he has done wrong and will be astonished by the negative expressions of emotions he encounters from people he has inadvertently offended

The Angry Eye

The Fire Wheel Eye

The description of the Fire Wheel Eye is one of the few occasions in this branch of face reading that colour is mentioned. Tradition states that the iris has a green, red or blue ring around it and that there are concentric circles of colour within the iris itself. This eye configuration is very similar to the Angry Eye but if anything the person is even quicker to anger. People who possess this type of eye are constantly on the edge of fury and it wouldn't take much to tip the balance. However these people are extremely alert, possibly a little paranoid and some would say that they are constantly looking for someone or something to offend them. They are very aware of the strengths and weaknesses of those around them and will be very free with their criticisms.

The Sand Eye

The Sand Eye is notable for the flecks of yellowish colour within the iris (these do not make concentric circles). In the west, the Sand Eye is extremely common and is usually found in those with blue or even lighter eyes. Possessors of this type of eye are mentally acute and extremely alert to the world around them. They tend to be great talkers and enjoy nothing more than a good discussion. This type of person could be described as mercurial, quick thinking, quick talking and never short of an answer. They excel in debate because they have an innate capacity to spot to flaws in an opposing argument and counter them with a display of devastating wit. However this capacity for argument can degenerate into a quarrelsome pattern of behaviour if it is not controlled.

The Fire Wheel Eye

The Sand Eye

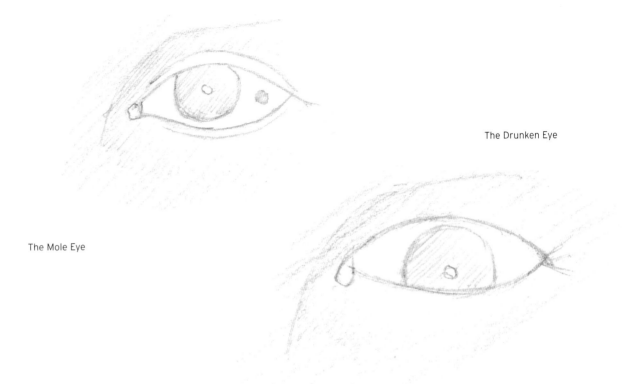

The Drunken Eye

The Mole Eye

The Mole Eye

If a small spot of dark colour is found in the white of the eye then this type is described as a Mole Eye. Traditionally this is not considered a good sign because even though the possessor of this type of eye is likely to have periods of good fortune, they will not last. This is a shame because this type of person has a capacity for great enjoyment of the good life. He will also be generally benevolent to those around him and have a kind heart. However it is this very charitable disposition that will lead him to ruin unless he is very careful indeed. It is likely that he will be surrounded by people who are more than willing to take advantage of his good nature.

The Drunken Eye

These eyes tend to be similar to the four White Eye, having the iris in the lower portion of the eyeball. However, the area surrounding the iris will tend to be reddish or yellowish rather than white. These eyes have a lethargic look hinting at heavy upper eyelids and any crow's feet present will be made up of many short wrinkles. However, in contrast to its name, the possessor of this type of eye will literally have a roving eye. The sexual nature will be very strong and indeed, the possessor of Drunken Eyes will tend to be extremely attractive to the opposite sex. In terms of general luck though this configuration is not so promising. There will be periods when all plans will go wrong and a series of mishaps and crises will occur. Tradition states that there is little that can be done about this except to cultivate patience and hold to the belief that this time of ill fortune will eventually pass.

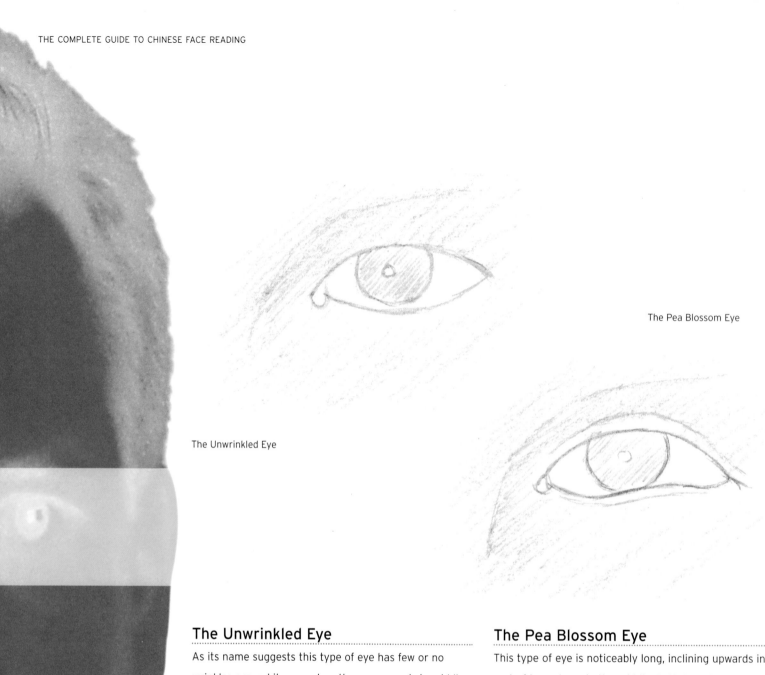

The Pea Blossom Eye

The Unwrinkled Eye

The Unwrinkled Eye

As its name suggests this type of eye has few or no wrinkles around it even when the possessor is in middle or old age. This type of eye is smooth and rounded at the edges having no angles at all in its outer portion. The general aspect of this eye suggests youthfulness and indeed it is an indicator of an active intelligence. Its general interpretation is one of eloquence and charm. This person's powers of persuasion could lead them into a career as a salesman, public relations or spokesperson. However, it is this very gift of the gab that could also lead them into trouble. Their romantic life especially is prone to disruption simply because this gift can so easily be turned to seduction. In short, a person with an Unwrinkled Eye is likely to have serial relationships at best but concurrent ones are far more likely.

The Pea Blossom Eye

This type of eye is noticeably long, inclining upwards in a sort of bow-shape in the middle. Both the iris and the white of the eye are somewhat cloudy or shadowed. The Pea Blossom eye is said to denote a person who is very cautious indeed. He is a keen observer of human nature who has become something of a cynic, a fact that is often completely masked by charm. One clue to spotting this type lies in the fact that those with Pea Blossom Eyes will rarely look straight at you while they are trying to work out your motives. However, they are also very likely to be extremely talented and often excel in the arts or in careers that require personal flair. This type is also likely to be extremely popular and have an active social life and many lifelong friends. Some of these friends will be old lovers because the Pea Blossom person has a capacity to retain affection even when passion is spent.

The Elephant Eye

Like an elephant, possessors of this type of eye will have many wrinkles both above and below the eye. The eye itself will tend to be narrow and long with an aspect of wisdom about it. This is considered to be the eye type of the sage, a person of experience and perception. Like the elephant, this type of person has a long memory and is also kind, compassionate and helpful to those in need. In fact, a person with the eyes of the mighty pachyderm will tend to go to great lengths to give assistance to one who has stirred his sympathies. The inner nature is creative and also very sensitive. The Elephant Eye type will be enthusiastic and full of humour.

The Lion Eye

The gaze of a person with the eyes of a lion is direct, straight and unflinching. The iris is high like that of the Wolf Eye and there will be few or no lines on the lower eyelid. However there will be several strong lines on the upper. People possessing the eyes of the king of the beasts are usually very career-minded. They take what they do very seriously indeed and cannot bear to be made the butt of jokes or even tolerate light-hearted banter. Their diligence and ambition brings great rewards. They will achieve positions of respectability and responsibility. In general their judgement will be flawless and they will tend to be looked up to as examples and role models.

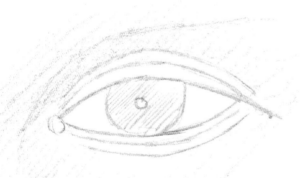

The Lion Eye

The Elephant Eye

The Tiger Eye

Similar to the Lion's Eye, those of the tiger have a more golden hue. The crow's feet at the edge will be short, faint and rather scattered. There are few or no creases beneath the eye yet there will be one strong line on the upper eyelid. This type of eye denotes a forceful character with strong attitudes and opinions. Other people will tend to look to the Tiger's Eye type for guidance and leadership. There is, however an occasional pressing need for solitude and indeed there will be times when circumstances dictate working and living alone. Fortunately those with the eye of the tiger are happy in their own company. This type may also be eccentric with an unusual lifestyle and quirky interests.

The Crane Eye

The eyes of the crane are big, rounded, long and as clear as a sunlit pool. The iris will be centrally located. There may be two or more creases on the upper eyelid. This type of eye denotes a person of unimpeachable integrity. Their honesty takes the form of open and forthright statements simply because this type of person cannot stand deviousness in any way. The Crane Eye shows that its possessor is likely to be generally fortunate throughout life and will win steadfast and loyal friends and allies. There is a deeply compassionate nature and a love of the natural world.

The Crane Eye

The Tiger Eye

The Eagle Eye

The eyes of the eagle are long and fairly narrow. The iris is located high on the eyeball and there may be a yellowish tinge to the eye. One long crease is usually visible on the upper eyelid, but beneath there are no long wrinkles at all. People with Eagle Eyes are loners. By their own choice they tend to prefer to live or work in solitude. They see the world their own way and will live their lives according to their own terms. They do not take kindly to being dictated to or to 'toeing the line'. Although they will be fond of their family and their friends they will tend to keep them at arm's length and will not turn to them for assistance even when they are in trouble.

The Goose Eye

The Goose Eye tends to be rather long although since it is so well rounded it appears to be in proportion. The iris is centrally placed and may possess a golden hue. There are definite and noticeable creases both above and below the eye. People in possession of Goose Eyes are pretty relaxed. They have a light-hearted view of life and an easy, outgoing personality. They make friends easily, and if some fall by the wayside so what, there'll be a few more along in a minute. A certain lack of ambition is unlikely to worry them unduly simply because they will tend to be happy the way things are. Although Goose Eye people may not achieve the highest status that they are capable of, their lives will be contented and fulfilling.

The Eagle Eye

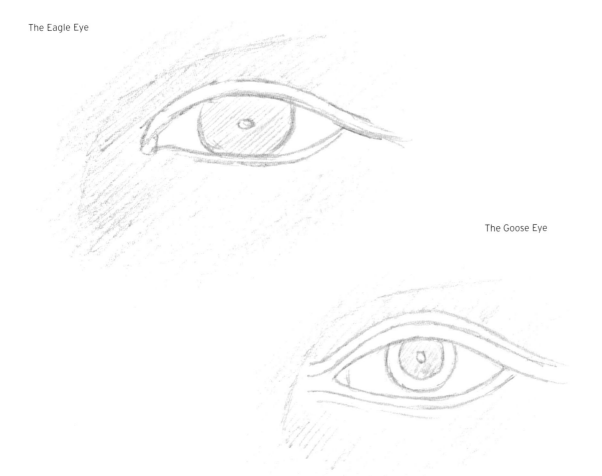

The Goose Eye

The Swallow Eye

The Horse Eye

The Swallow Eye

Swallow eyes are deep-set, framed by a long crease both above and below them. The eyes will give the impression of sharpness and will be noticeably bright and clear. The Swallow Eye could also be described as being elegant and rather beautiful. This type of person will hold a promise to be a sacred trust, and indeed will win respect and admiration for the way he keeps his word even when breaking it would be in his best interest. Unfortunately this is not the type of eye that indicates wealth or status but nevertheless denotes a lifestyle that is comfortable and satisfying.

The Horse Eye

This type of eye bulges slightly and is rather watery. There will be many folds of skin and creases on the lower eyelid while the upper lid is generally wrinkle free with a soft and delicate appearance. Crow's feet at the outer edge of the eye will be inclined downwards. This is the eye of a hard worker who perseveres through thick and thin, often struggling against overwhelming odds. Like the carthorse, he continues his thankless task through all weathers and in all conditions. Unfortunately this person may not receive the rewards for his efforts that are justly his. In short, this person will have a life that has more than its fair share of difficulties in his career and in private. Nevertheless he will not lose heart and will shows a courage that puts more obviously gifted people to shame.

The Lamb Eye

These eyes tend to be dark with a yellowish tinge to both the whites and the iris. It is also possible that there are concentric lines within the pupil. The upper eyelid will have noticeable fold of skin while the lower eyelid will not. In addition the lower eyelid will be flat and have thin, delicate skin marked with lines. The crow's feet at the outer edge will be faint, thin and fairly scattered. Lamb Eyes are the mark of someone who is always busy. This is a hard worker who leaves himself little time to enjoy the fruits of his labours. In addition to this lack of opportunity for fun, incidents beyond this person's control will conspire to ensure that he is always in demand. Help from others is not often in evidence, even when one would assume that it would be freely given. Those with Lamb Eyes have to rely on themselves because they learn early on that they can't rely on anyone else.

The Ox Eye

The eye of the ox is rather large and rounded but it does not bulge. Both the iris and the whites are very clear indeed. This is the mark of a person who is gentle both in manner and attitude. Very forgiving, the ox-eyed person will overlook past wrongs and readily give offenders a second or even a third chance to redeem themselves. Although this person's feelings run deep it is unlikely that there will be any emotional outbursts. If you spot a person with Ox Eyes take special note of the crow's feet at the outer edges. If they incline upwards then this is likely to be an extremely trustworthy character who will never let you down. If downwards then the passivity of this ox is such that promises will be made with every intention of keeping them but little will ever be done.

The Ox Eye

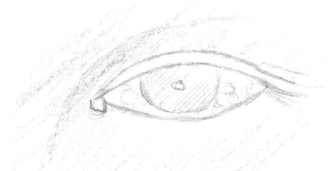

The Lamb Eye

The Pig Eye

The heavy coarse-lidded Pig Eye is said to be dark and muddy. These eyes tend to be quite small, and peer suspiciously about them. This kind of eye is not the most fortunate to possess. People of this type are said to be tempestuous and irritable, sharp tongued and impulsive. Obviously insecure, they try to bolster a weak self-image with constant and often inaccurate criticisms of others. In consequence people with Pig Eyes often unnecessarily make enemies when in reality they are their own worst enemy. If such a person would try to relax a little and think before they speak their lives would be so much easier.

The Pig Eye

The Monkey Eye

The Monkey Eye

The Monkey Eye is small and fairly short in length. The iris is positioned towards the top of the eye. There is also a distinct crease or fold on the upper eyelid that curves down sharply towards the outer corner of the eye and may even extend beyond it. As the name implies possessors of Monkey Eyes are ever curious and are noted for their multiplicity of skills. These people have an optimistic and outgoing character and they are capable of great courage in times of difficulty. Their bright, inventive and cheerful characters will win respect and admiration from those who are not so bold. According to Chinese tradition possessors of Monkey Eyes are, like their namesakes, said to have a particular fondness for fruit.

THE EYEBROWS

The eyebrows are one of the most mobile features of the face. Along with the eyes and mouth they rise and fall with changes of mood and are most expressive of the character. Without the visual stimuli that the eyebrows provide it would be almost impossible to detect the emotional state or mental attitude of a given person. This is perhaps the reason that Queen Elizabeth I of England and the Mona Lisa shaved theirs off to highlight an enigmatic aspect.

The eyebrows are one of the five vital features of the face and form the border between the upper or celestial zone and the central or zone of self-will. In terms of the age positions of the face the eyebrows relate to the early thirties. The outer extremities of the far right and left correspond to 30 and 31 respectively. The inner tips of the eyebrows are allocated the ages 32 on the right and 33 on the left.

In ancient Chinese tradition well over thirty different shapes are described, although for general purposes we can content ourselves with defining twenty-one basic ones. However, before we move onto examining these we should pause to consider the interpretation of the various types of hair growth within the eyebrow itself without being unduly worried about the individual shapes just yet.

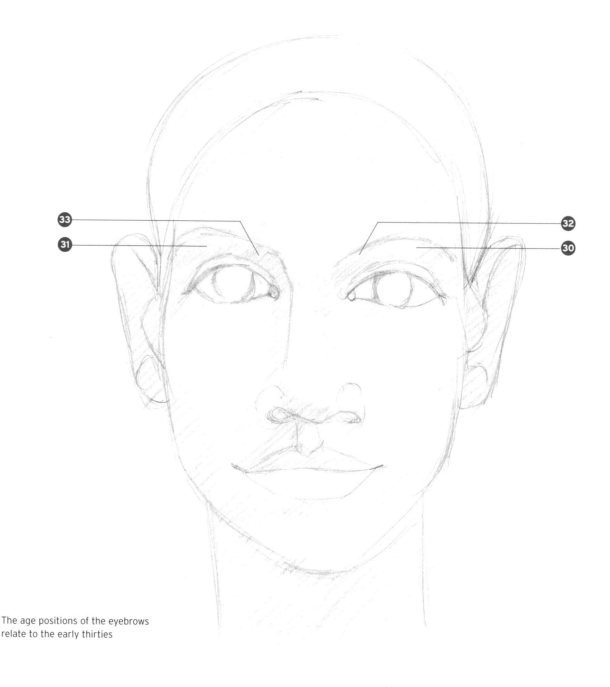

The age positions of the eyebrows relate to the early thirties

The Prominent Eyebrow Ridge

An eyebrow ridge that is well defined and strong denotes a personality that is courageous and individualistic. People with this feature are often stubborn, being convinced that they are always right… even when they are undoubtedly wrong! This can lead to long drawn out arguments. On the plus side, this type of person will be an asset to any cause to which he espouses himself. The feature also denotes excellent powers of concentration.

Upward-growth of Eyebrow Hairs

This feature is another indicator of courage but it can also show a tendency to have a foul, and easily aroused temper. Tactlessness is an obvious character trait of this kind of hair growth. The possessor of this type of eyebrow will often speak before he thinks and act without forethought.

Downward-growth of Eyebrow Hairs

This feature often indicates a lack of confidence. People possessing this feature are often nervous and try to avoid confrontations at any cost. There is also a tendency to shift blame and not face up to the consequences of actions. Relationships can also be a problem area due to a lack of self-esteem that puts extra pressure on the partner.

Eyebrows with Mixed Growth

In Chinese tradition this is known as 'hairs that embrace' or charmingly 'cuddling hairs'. The hairs at the top of the eyebrow grown downwards while those at the base grow in an upward direction. This is the mark of a worrier, of someone who is plagued by anxieties that are often totally unnecessary.

A fiery temper and an impulsive nature are shown by the upward growth of eyebrow hair

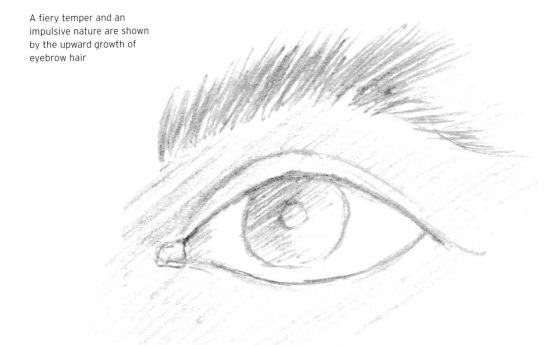

Scattered Directions of Hair Growth

This feature is generally found in thick eyebrows where all the hair grows in different directions. This is the mark of someone who has to cope with unexpected difficulties and setbacks throughout life. Tradition states that possessors of this feature will not easily win favour from those in positions of power and authority.

Clear, Thin Eyebrows

Delicate eyebrows such as the thin and clear type are indicative of someone who has a rather placid, calm and untroubled character. This sort of person does not like to have too many demands placed upon them but when duty calls they will cope with it with efficiency and speed.

The Twenty One Shapes of the Eyebrow

The Long Eyebrow

This type of eyebrow has a gentle curve and extends beyond the edge of the eye. It may in fact extend beyond both sides of the eye and in some cases these eyebrows meet. Despite the superstition that you should never trust someone whose eyebrows meet in the middle, this feature indicates a keen intellect and eloquent speech. It is also said to foretell a happy and prosperous middle age.

The Short Eyebrow

The hairs on this type of eyebrow tend to be rather coarse and uneven in length. As its name implies, this eyebrow does not extend the full length of the eye. This feature can indicate someone who comes from a fairly small family or one who has little contact with his relatives. He may fully intend to keep in touch but arguments and bad feeling can sour familial relationships.

The Big Eyebrow

This type of eyebrow extends the full length of the eye, is wide with strong hair growth. This feature adds up to courage and tenacity. People with a wide eyebrow are never afraid to speak up or to make their feelings known. In relationships, the possessor of the big eyebrow is likely to be the dominant partner. If found in combination with a strong brow ridge, it indicates that the person will be very formidable indeed.

The Clannish Eyebrow

This type of eyebrow resembles the appearance of the Chinese character for the number one. Its hair growth is thick and the eyebrow is of medium length but should extend a little beyond the edge of the eye. The most notable feature is that the hair roots are quite visible in this type. The eyebrow denotes someone from a large and extended family. The reputation of this person is likely to be exemplary and a long stable relationship is forecast.

The Loner Eyebrow

The shape of this eyebrow resembles the letter Y or the
Chinese character for the number eight. The hair growth
is rather thin. This is a feature found in people who like
to be solitary. Such a person is often ill at ease
in the company of others. However he is
a hard worker who will make the most
of opportunities. It also foretells a
long life and contentment.

The Ghost Eyebrow

Although similar to the Loner Eyebrow, the Ghost type
descends lower to the bridge of the nose and is more
curved. The hair tends to grow upwards. This is a person
who finds it very difficult to trust other people. He
conceals his feelings and thoughts and can be
rather antagonistic.

The Rolling Eyebrow

As the name implies, the eyebrow hairs are thick and curly, usually inclining towards the outer edge of the eye. This is an unusual feature most often seen on the faces of military leaders and politicians. It denotes a capacity to take control and be readily accepted in a leadership role.

The Broom Eyebrow

No one could miss this type of eyebrow. It is thick, long and pretty wild with scattered hairs towards the outer edge. The wildness of the eyebrow can reflect the wildness of the person who possesses it. Although it is likely that he comes from a large family, it is unlikely that he keeps in close contact with them. He is an individualist who requires great understanding when he is in a relationship. This is not an indicator of wealth but he will never be short of money.

The Little Broom Eyebrow

Almost identical to the Broom Eyebrow, this type is short and does not extend to the edge of the eye. This feature indicates a person who is exceptional at talking himself in and out of trouble. Tempestuous and impatient, he is probably difficult to live with and comes from a somewhat neurotic family background.

The Beautiful Eyebrow

The Beautiful Eyebrow is rather long and delicately curved. The hairs tend to be fine and grow in the same upward direction. This type of eyebrow may be high or low but is nevertheless rather lovely. This is an indicator of trustworthiness and honour. The possessor of this type of eyebrow will keep his word and be discriminating in judgement. Fair play is of first importance to this person and he will be a skilled arbitrator in all disputes. The Beautiful Eyebrow is a sign of good fortune.

The Mortal Eyebrow

This eyebrow is very short, wide and thick. Its hairs tend to be rather coarse and bushy. This is another eyebrow type that marks out a loner, however this person will enjoy company but most often prefers to live alone. Close friendships and lasting relationships will be formed but not necessarily any domestic arrangements. There may be a separation from parents and the rest of the family and little support will come from that direction. Any offspring will be born in later life.

The Sword Eyebrow

This type of eyebrow tends to be rather high on the brow and like the blade which give it its name is flat, long, straight and wide becoming thicker at the outside edge. All the hairs will tend to grow in the same upward direction. This is the mark of an astute person, one who has wisdom. A natural organiser and leader, this eyebrow is the mark of someone successful in business. The eyebrow is also said to indicate longevity and a large family.

The Knife Eyebrow

The shape of this eyebrow suggests the blade of a knife or a dagger. The hairs of this type tend to be coarse. This is the mark of an astute person who will gain great advantages in life. However there will be a tendency to always seek the easy route. Possibly this person is something of a boaster.

The Rising Eyebrow

Shaped like the knife or the sword (see above), the Rising Eyebrow is also somewhat akin to that of Mr Spock of 'Star Trek' fame, soaring diagonally upwards from the bridge of the nose. This feature shows amazing determination and a refusal to admit defeat in any circumstances. It is the mark of someone who is extremely dominant and can be aggressive or at least argumentative. This is someone who will bend heaven and earth to win, and win big! Success comes early to this type and tends to continue throughout life. Personal relationships and family links may suffer as a result of this relentless drive.

The Weeping Eyebrow

The opposite of the Rising Eyebrow is the Weeping Eyebrow. It too has a diagonal slope but this time rises from the outer edge of the eye inclining toward the middle. This aspect gives its possessor a rather sad or mournful look. This person is enigmatic. It is difficult to work out what he thinks or feels. However you can be sure that he is very shrewd and will make the most of all opportunities. He is clever and fast thinking and will not be afraid to offend if that gets him to the top by the fastest possible route.

The Willow Leaf Eyebrow

This is a curved, delicate eyebrow with fairly tangled hairs. This feature indicates a person who is open, honest and friendly. He has an excellent intellect and a very lively, mercurial mind. There is a great enjoyment of social life and he will be a popular companion to people from all walks of life. Influential friends will help him achieve success. People with Willow Leaf Eyebrows don't usually start a family until later in life.

The New Moon Eyebrow

This type of eyebrow rises high above the eye, gently curving like the crescent of the new moon. Tradition holds that the hairs are fine and glossy as if with an inner light, all growing in the same direction. This is an indication that this person is very compassionate and thoughtful. Honesty and trustworthiness are notable. Family life in both early and later life is likely to be happy. The New Moon Eyebrow is a sure sign of fidelity in marriage.

The Longevity Eyebrow

This eyebrow is wide with a significant lengthening of the hair at the tail end. Often these end hairs will curve downwards beyond the edge of the eye. The hairs are said to be rather glossy and dark. As the name implies this is a fortunate type of eyebrow to possess. It foretells a long, happy and successful life. Its possessor is likely to be artistically creative and a particularly gifted writer. Charming and friendly the owner of the Longevity Eyebrow is also said to be sexually alluring.

The Dragon Eyebrow

The Dragon Eyebrow rises in a straight diagonal line for most of its length and then slopes downwards past the outer edge of the eye. This type is said to be well shaped and elegant. The hairs are fine and glossy. The possessor of this type of eyebrow is very clever with a keen business sense and well respected by friends and associates. Intolerant of injustice this person will not be afraid to speak up for a cause. The Dragon Eyebrow is also an indicator of wealth. The family of origin is likely to be large and far-flung.

The Silkworm Eyebrow

This type of eyebrow gently rises on the forehead. It is smooth, has an even shape while the hairs are smooth, silky and somewhat curled. This is the mark of someone who is well trusted and popular. Its possessor will be quick-witted and capable of making the best out of any situation. Self-discipline is also a strong character strait. The Silkworm Eyebrow predicts opportunities that could lead to fame and fortune.

The Lion Eyebrow

The Lion type of eyebrow is curly along its curved length. It is wide and thick having an appearance of strength. Although the hair is dense the roots will still be visible. Although this eyebrow shape can make its possessor look constantly irritated it is actually a mark of a thoughtful individual. Generosity of spirit is also a characteristic and this will win affection and respect. However there may be marital difficulties and domestic quarrels. The Lion Eyebrow is also said to indicate longevity.

THE BROW

The brow or forehead forms the Heavenly or Celestial area of the face. It is also considered to be one of the 'five mountains' of the face. It is represented by the Red Bird of the South and is under the governance of the fire element. In the symbolism of face reading this fiery aspect represents the intellectual capabilities and character traits associated with the more cerebral side of life. This may be revealed by the height and breadth of the forehead as well as any distinguishing features such as grooves and wrinkles that may be found upon it.

The Hairline

The first thing to note when examining the brow is the shape of the hairline. This falls into five basic categories, each associated with one of the five elements of Chinese tradition.

The Long Straight Hairline

This feature is often found in conjunction with a face shape that is square or rectangular and is associated with the earth element. It signifies a character that is rational and methodical. The possessor of this feature commonly thinks that there is a place for everything, and that everything (and sometimes everyone) should be in its place. Mostly straightforward and conventional, people with this style of hair growth can be somewhat unimaginative and plodding.

The Short Straight Hairline

Although similar to the longer version above, those with a short straight hairline are rather self-obsessed and possibly have repressed desires. This pattern of hair growth is said to point to irritability and narrow views. It may also reveal an unhappy childhood and a desperate need for affection. It is also considered likely that such a person will have many serial relationships and will be generally anxious and prone to black moods. This sort of hairline is symbolically connected to the metal element.

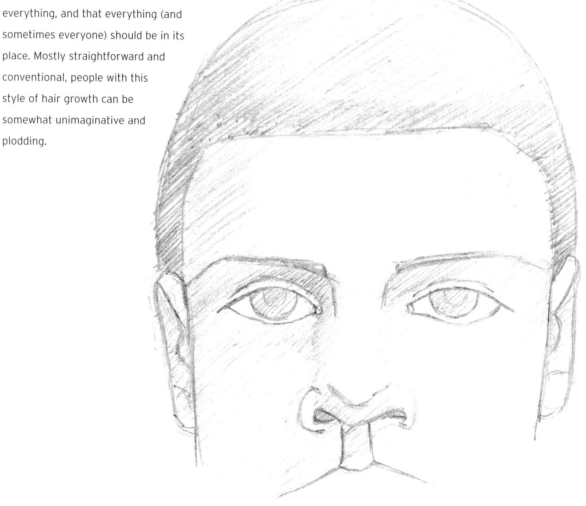

The Peaked Hairline

A hairline that rises to a point towards the crown of the head is associated with the fire element and signifies a strong desire to rise to exalted heights in the world. It may also show that this person wishes to separate himself from his origins and to recreate his life anew. This person will have great intelligence but may be markedly intolerant of other people's views, and remarkably fixed in his own.

The Rounded Hairline

This pattern of hair growth is associated with the element water and, like that most changeable of elements, its possessor may be fickle. If it is connected to the water face shape, then overly imaginative and superstitious attitudes are to be expected. If this hairline is combined with a face shape other than water it brings more positive traits to the fore. These include a powerful intuition and a more open expression of feeling.

The Widow's Peak

A hairline that points downwards towards the nose in an M shape is connected to the exuberant wood element. It reveals a sensitive and creative nature. Its possessor may be generally shy, yet desire public acclaim. It may also point to an inner feeling of superiority to those around him. The possessor of a widow's peak does not like to be responsible for other people and many with this feature prefer to live alone. In many ways, this sort of hairline reveals someone who is very gifted but prone to self-doubt. Commonly self-indulgent, some with this feature become vain and narcissistic.

Even and Uneven Hairlines

Before we move on to the forehead proper, there is one other factor to be considered when examining the hairline. This is that any hairline, high or low, can be even or uneven. If it is even then this is likely to be a person who tends to stick to the straight and narrow, one who will not step outside the conventions of his society. However if the hair growth is uneven then an element of rebellion creeps into the character and this person will often find his views, beliefs and actions at odds with the world around him.

Receding Hairlines

It is an unfortunate fact that, with age, men's hairlines in particular are subject to a worrying change. So when assessing the shape of the hair growth it is important not to overestimate the height of the forehead due to hair loss. Loss of hair does not increase the height of the forehead and the old line of hair growth can be detected on close examination.

The Height of the Forehead

Even in popular imagination, the height of the forehead
is considered to be one of the main indicators of
intelligence. Someone whose forehead is prominent and
noticeable is considered to be more intelligent than a
person whose brow is low. This belief gives rise to the
description of an intellectual as 'highbrow'. Indeed,
practitioners of Chinese face reading also share this
common view, and also add that forehead height is an
indicator of wit.

The forehead height should be measured from the point
between the eyebrows to the hairline. Ideally, this
distance should be equal to the length of the nose and
the distance from the tip of the nose to the tip of the
chin. This is known as the classical proportion. If
however the height of the forehead is less than either of
those distances then it reveals a lack of intelligence,
forethought and charisma. It may also point to
difficulties in getting along with others. Working and
social relationships in particular may be troublesome,
and punctuated by quarrels.

The Width of the Forehead

This distance is measured from temple to temple about
5cm (1 inch) above the eyebrow line. This measurement
is symbolic of the breadth of vision. If the forehead is
narrow then its possessor will likewise be limited by
preconceptions, prejudices and intolerance. Conversely, if
the forehead is broad, a mind open to new concepts,
libertarian principles and understanding is indicated.

Pronounced forehead
above eyebrows

Pronounced forehead
in the the middle

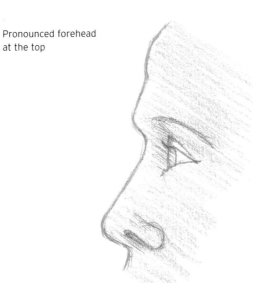

Pronounced forehead
at the top

The Three Regions of the Brow

In addition to the hairline, the height and the width of the forehead there is another indicator present, and this is the celestial area of the face. This is the division of the brow into three horizontal zones relating to mental functions. The topmost of these zones is dedicated to the imagination. The middle area represents the faculty of memory while the lower zone (just above the eyebrow line) symbolises the powers of observation. Any prominence, bulge, scar or mark on the forehead will fall into one of these areas and will reveal either problems or advantages connected to these mental faculties. For instance, should the area above the eyebrows be fuller and more prominent than any other area on the forehead then the perceptive abilities will be heightened. A forehead that bulges in the middle will indicate an exceptional memory while one that protrudes at the top just beneath the hairline will indicate an excellent imagination and the potential for exaggeration and fantasy.

The three distinct regions
of the brow

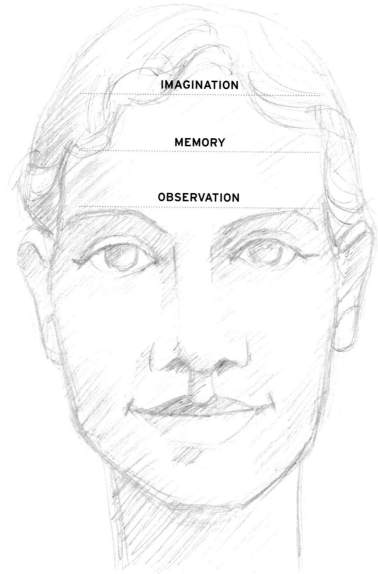

IMAGINATION

MEMORY

OBSERVATION

Horizontal Creases

Many people have horizontal creases on the forehead and these too can provide extra information. Strictly speaking, Chinese face reading does not take these into account, but this is not the case in the ancient western art of physiognomy. According to this discipline, the forehead has a similar meaning to the first house of the horoscope chart, revealing the image and the impact one will make on society. There are seven possible creases to be found on the brow and these are symbolised by the seven traditional planets of astrology. The highest crease is said to have the nature of grim dour Saturn, optimistic Jupiter governs the one immediately below it, aggressive Mars follows with the crease of the regal sun below that. The sun crease occupies the central line of the forehead while amorous Venus, eloquent Mercury and the domestically inclined Moon crease are found below it in that order.

Of course not everyone has all seven on their foreheads so it is difficult to spot which of the lines are rep-

resented. Some people have no creases at all, a situation that a physiognomist would regard as a sign of a distinct lack of character. Possessing all seven isn't a good sign either because it leads to confusion and melancholy. The best omen is the presence of three parallel creases, which grant good luck and are known as the 'Three Fortunes'.

In practice, though, the presence of a well-defined horizontal crease across the middle of the brow is a sign of high achievements, a good reputation, and, in some cases, of fame. It also denotes a strong constitution, optimism, energy and drive. These are all apt interpretations of the line of the sun. Note should also be taken if a crease is low to the eyebrow. This will be the line of Mercury and reveals swiftness of thought, eloquence, wit and an ability to write fluently.

If any of the horizontal creases are frayed, broken or very faint they can harm the fortunes by marring the imagination, the memory or the powers of observation, depending on the zone of the brow in which they lie.

This relatively rare crease pattern resembles a Chinese character meaning 'king' and is very fortunate indeed

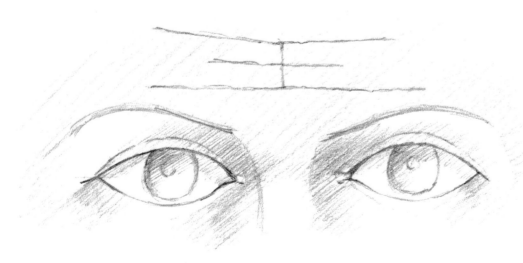

Vertical Creases

With vertical creases rising from the top of the nose we are back to the oriental traditions. A lot of store is placed on these markings because they are said to be very significant in revealing the course of an individual's fate.

The Single Vertical Crease

This solitary line rising from the top of the nose signifies great powers of concentration. This is a person who will rise to a position of prominence through his own diligence and vision. However, there is also a warning given when this feature is present - the line may also indicate selfishness, anxiety and a tendency to make enemies who will engineer financial troubles. This feature is also called the 'Hanging Needle'. If another line branches off from the Hanging Needle, the outlook becomes much more positive and fortunate. However, should the Hanging Needle be crossed by transverse lines, the outlook is explosive because this person is not only single-minded but ruthless and prone to violent outbursts.

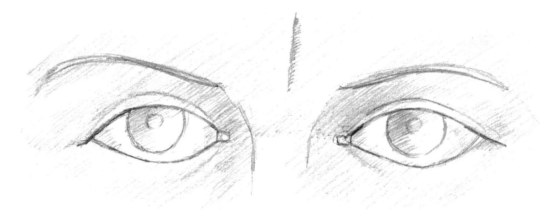

Inverted Creases

If the creases incline towards each other and then bend back on themselves it reveals a person who lacks courage in his convictions. It is a sign of someone who is prone to attacks of anxiety and even though he is self-centred he also lacks confidence.

Parallel Creases

This is a common feature found on people who have a
balanced mind, who are willing to listen to both sides of
an argument and who give their judgements accordingly.
However, the inclination of these creases can affect the
interpretation.

Wavering creases

Wavering Creases

If the parallel creases meander up the brow like twin
rivulets there will be a great deal of uncertainty and lack
of purpose. The possessor of this feature will find it
difficult to establish himself in a lasting role and may
wander from job to job, relationship to relationship. This
is considered to be a very unfortunate feature and can
indicate someone who puts himself in personal danger.

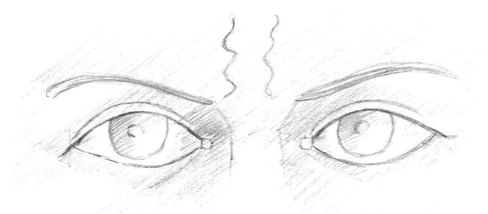

Inward Sloping Creases

If the parallel creases slope inwards, towards each other,
the character will be more self-centred, although without
the unflinching sense of purpose that goes with a single
line. Relationships are a danger area for someone with
this feature because the 'me first' attitude will eventually
become very wearing to the partner.

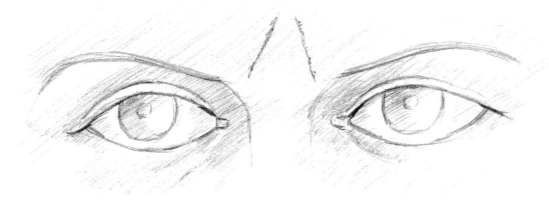

Crossed Vertical Creases

If transverse lines cross the parallel creases it is an indication of an irritable nature and a great deal of inner tension. People with this feature often find themselves unable to sustain a worthwhile relationship and are therefore sad, which in turn, adds to their original irritability.

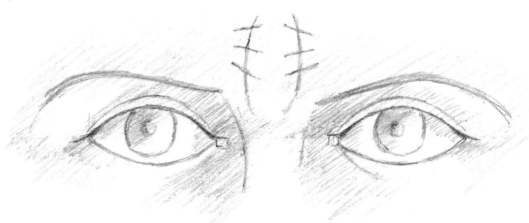

Trident-like Creases

If the two outer lines of a three-crease formation incline outwards, the indications are fortunate but marred somewhat by an unpleasant, peevish and rather self-indulgent personality.

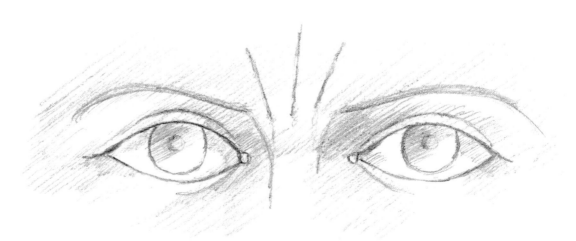

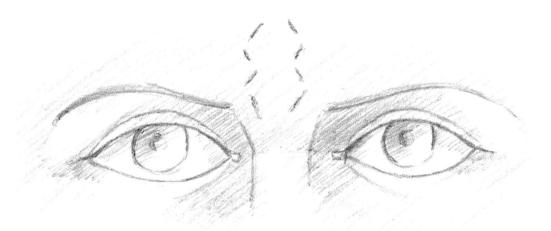

Broken Vertical Creases

Vertical creases which are broken or faint, being more a collection of short lines progressing up the forehead, foretell many troubles in the person's twenties. However this need not necessarily be a bad thing, but rather a character-building experience, the misfortunes of which can be rectified in later life.

Three Vertical Creases

This is a very fortunate feature indicating that the possessor of these creases will rise to a position of honour and authority. In many cases it is also a sign of fame and a sign that this person will be known to many people and will also benefit from his celebrity.

Three Broken, Wavering Creases

This is a very bad sign, indicating ruthlessness and a desire for high achievements that cannot be gained by honest means. Traditionally this feature indicates a criminal temperament.

TOP: A a broken, wavering crease pattern represents dishonesty and is clearly not considered to be a fortunate feature, BOTTOM: More that four vertical creases, whether broken or straight, is thought to carry negative meaning

Four or more Vertical Creases

The presence of four or even more vertical creases is not a favourable omen no matter how well-formed, straight or defined they happen to be. This formation indicates severe restlessness and lack of direction. Although the possessor of this feature is likely to be multitalented, he will jump from one project to another without finishing anything, and thus will waste his efforts on frivolous and wasteful endeavours. The four-crease formation does not bode well for such a person's future. He may become a wanderer with nowhere in particular to go. The abuse of alcohol or drugs is often associated with this feature.

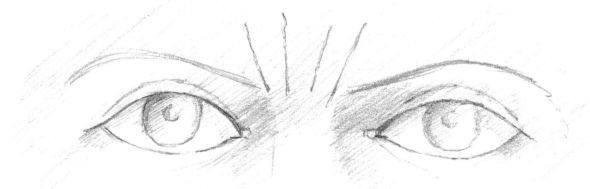

The Chinese Characters of the Brow

Although the chances of finding a combination of vertical and horizontal grooves that form a Chinese character on the brow are slim, to say the least, they do have their place in traditional interpretation. The first formation resembles the Chinese character for 'king' while the second means 'mountain'. It is claimed that if you meet someone with either of these patterns upon his forehead he is destined for great things. He will be respected by all, friends, family and strangers, and will achieve prosperity and make an indelible mark on the world.

TOP: It is considered fortunate to possess a crease pattern resembling the Chinese character for 'king'. A person with this pattern will gain respect and authority
BOTTOM: A crease pattern that resembles the Chinese symbol for 'mountain' is another fortunate feature signifying high achievements and prosperity

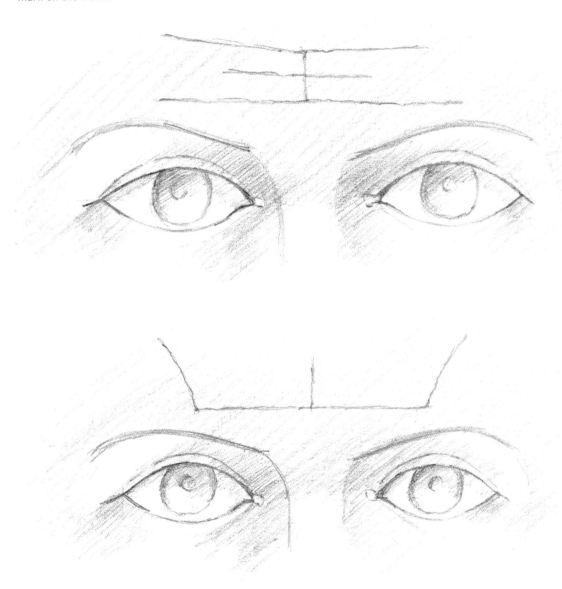

THE EARS

Even though the other features of the face, or indeed the head and the body have numerous individual characteristics, their variety and forms do not compare with the number and types of ear that are possible. Indeed, before the discovery and use of finger printing, it was suggested that suspected criminals be identified by ear shape. This is a fact that testifies to their uniqueness. However, apart from their use in criminology, the shape and positioning of the ears have much to do with an assessment of intelligence.

In the art of face reading the ears are accorded a singular importance, emphasised by the fact that the hairstyles of many people serve to hide these otherwise revealing features. After all, one really has to know another very well indeed to allow them a close examination of one's ears. Be that as it may, the first thing to note about the ears is their positioning relative to the eyebrows and the tip of the nose. This is as well as taking into account whether the ears are set far back on the head or are placed in a forward position close to the cheekbones.

In general terms, the further back that the ears are set on the head, the more intelligent their possessor. Ears which are close to the cheekbones indicate stupidity

Ear Positioning

The angle of the ears is determined by imagining a line starting at the eyebrows (the border between the Celestial and Human levels of the face) and then continuing through the ear-hole itself to the back of the head. According to the well-established rules the further back the ears are the more intelligent the person is likely to be. If the ear is set two thirds of the way back from the eyebrows it indicates an average intellect.

The Length of the Ear

The length of the ear is also an indicator of intelligence. A person who has ear tips which rise above the line of the eyebrows while also possessing lobes which extend below the line of the tip of the nose is very likely to be a genius of one sort or another. Needless to say most people will have ears that fall within these lines indicating an average mind. However, before any kind of final judgement of the matter can be reached one must also take note of the height and breadth of the forehead as well as the length and angle of the ear.

If the tops of the ears extend above the level of the eyebrow line, while the lobe is also at a higher level than the tip of the nose, then this person is likely to be a lively and entertaining exhibitionist. This is the sort of person who loves to be the centre of attention, one who is likely to have unconventional working methods and who will earn both praise and censure in equal measure.

If the tops of the ears are lower than the eyebrow line but the rest of the ear is nevertheless long, with the lobe reaching the level of the tip of the nose, then there will be a lack of attention to detail. This feature is the mark of a daydreamer who wastes time and neglects his duties. These traits will be emphasised if the ear is also rounded, soft and fleshy.

If the upper portion of the ear extends above the eyebrow level, while the lobe or ear-pearl is on exactly the same level as the nose tip, it is a sign of determination. This person will be successful by sheer dint of hard work and will be particularly fortunate if involved in a creative field.

If the ears are of different lengths, or indeed of different sizes it is an indication of misfortune. People who are unlucky enough to possess such a feature will find that their plans rarely come to fruition and they will be forced into making disadvantageous compromises again and again

The Symbolic Structure of the Ears

In the art of face reading the outline of the ear is called the Great Wheel. This is made up of three smaller wheels that mirror the threefold division of the face. Thus the upper portion of the ear is called the 'Heaven Wheel', the middle part, the 'Human Wheel' and the lobe or 'ear pearl' is also called the 'Earth Wheel'. In addition to this the interior of the ear is also called the 'Inner wheel'. The very centre point of these wheels is the ear hole itself, which actually and symbolically connects the complexities of the outside world to the convolutions of the brain.

The Ears and Childhood

According to the time-scale visible in the features in the traditions of Chinese face reading, the ears represent the early life. Working from the top of the ear to the lobe, the left ear covers the first to the seventh year of life while the right deals with the eighth to the fourteenth. The organs of hearing then reflect the impressionable and receptive period of childhood.

The View of the Ears from the Front

When looking at the face full on, the ears should be visible while still be close in to the head. Such a physical arrangement is said to reveal both a happy childhood and a contented and prosperous middle age. Ears that protrude often indicate someone who felt insecure as a child and this early anxiety may be a trait that never leaves him. In short it is the sign of a worrier. Particularly prominent ears (popularly, if rather cruelly, called 'jug-ears') are often found when the person has experienced a turbulent early life. The frustrations and repressed energies arising from this troublesome past will tend to stay with this person but they may be channelled into positive directions later on.

Ear Colouration

Chinese face reading takes particular note of the tones and colouration of the ears adding additional information to the interpretations of their shape and positioning.

An ear that is red or noticeably pink is yet another indication of a lively intelligence. A person with red ears is said to absorb information swiftly and with ease. He is also shrewd enough to use it to his best advantage.

Ears that are greyish in colouration indicate a talkative nature. However, if this skin tint is combined with small ears, then this is a person who finds it impossible to keep a secret, even when it is in his own best interests to do so. If grey areas suddenly appear on the ears it is likely that a period of misfortune is about to occur. Chinese tradition advises stoic patience to endure such a period.

Ears that are paler than the rest of the skin are a certain indication that this person's fame will spread, that he will achieve a great reputation and that he will be extremely successful.

The ear, like the face, is horizontally divided into the Heavenly, Human and Earthly regions. It also possesses inner and outer 'wheels' both centred on the ear hole

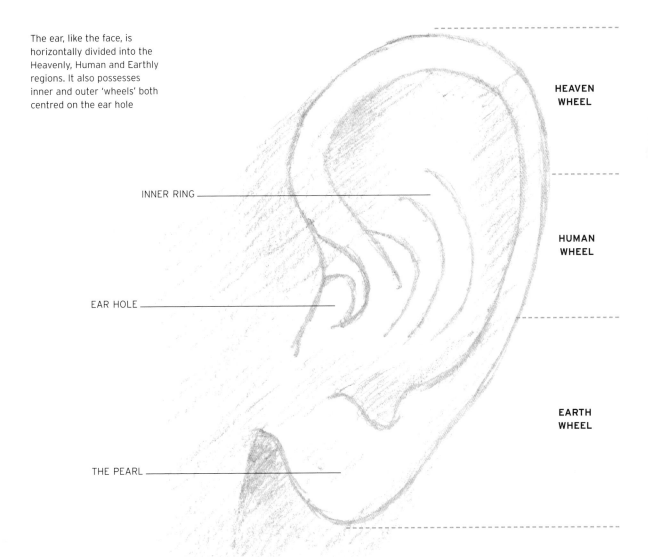

HEAVEN WHEEL

HUMAN WHEEL

EARTH WHEEL

INNER RING

EAR HOLE

THE PEARL

Traditional Types of Ear

As with other individual facial features such as the eyes, eyebrows and nose, tradition allocates extra interpretations to the various conformations of ears. The most important of these are set out here. People who are familiar with oriental mystical thought through Feng Shui or even Chinese horoscopes will recognise the first five types as being named after the five elements wood, fire, earth, metal and water.

The Wood Ear

The upper portion of this type of ear slopes upwards while the inner ring (usually the surround of the ear hole) grows beyond the outer wheel. The top of the ear, or Heaven Wheel is noticeably larger than the middle portion. The ear is thin and there is either a small lobe or no lobe at all. This is said to be an indicator that this person will be patient and persistent. This is a good thing since good fortune will not come to him easily and he will have to persevere to make a success of his life. However, the possessor of the Wood Ear will achieve his desires in the end. Tradition states that it also denotes a happy, healthy and prosperous old age. The chances of this happy fate are lessened if this ear type is combined with a face shape that is metal or earth in nature (see p.12-13).

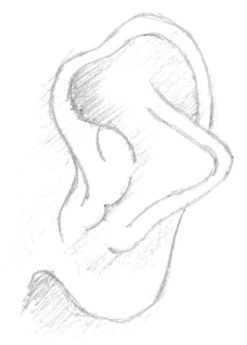

The Fire Ear

The Fire Ear

In the case of the fire ear, the top of the Heaven Wheel is pointed, and in common with the wood ear (see above) the inner ring extends beyond the outer wheel. This type of ear is not fleshy and feels rather hard to the touch. It is likely that the fire ear will possess a lobe. The fiery nature of this ear will be fully expressed in the character of the person who owns it. He is likely to be extremely headstrong and independent by nature and will find it almost impossible to accept criticism or advice. This is not a patient individual; neither is he an intellectual. He demands action and will sulk when his desires are thwarted. However, should the general face shape also be of the nature of the fire element then the chances for happiness and success are increased (p.11).

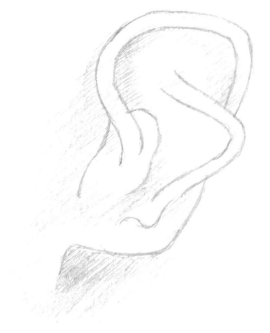

The Wood Ear

The Earth Ear

The earth ear is fleshy, quite full, fate and comparatively large. The lobe or ear-pearl will also be full and rounded, as indeed are both the outer and inner rings. The outer ring particularly will make up a large percentage of the ear itself. To possess this type of ear is considered a good omen. The Earth Ear signifies a long, happy and prosperous life. Personal loyalties to friends and family will stand the test of time and the possessor of this type of ear will win affection easily. The happiness and welfare of others will be as equally important to him as are his own. However, should the face shape be wood (see p.10), the outlook is not so good even though it is still favourable.

The Metal Ear

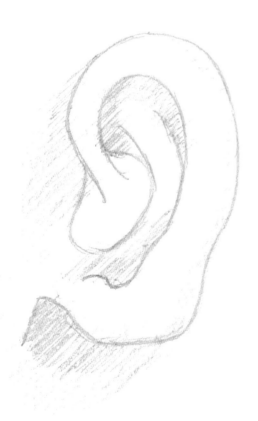

The Earth Ear

The Metal Ear

The Heaven Wheel or upper portion of the ear rises higher than the eyebrow line, and the outer and inner rings are so close that they almost touch. The general appearance of the ear is somewhat angular and the lobe is quite hard. The colour of the ear will also be paler than that of the rest of the face. The possessor of the Metal Ear is an intellectual with an active interest in the world around him and a highly developed curiosity. It often denotes someone who is creatively talented as well as foretelling career success and the gaining of wealth. However, it can show someone who in pursuit of his own personal gain (either intellectual or monetary) will sacrifice personal relationships. Family links in particular may become strained. Ill fortune is forecast if this type of ear is found in combination with a face shape that is wood in nature (p.10).

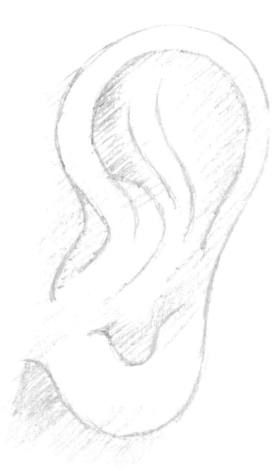

The Water Ear

The Chess Ear

This type of ear is rather small and well rounded. It also tends to be hard to the touch and quite thick. As with the Metal and Water Ears, the Chess Ear is lighter in colour than the rest of the complexion and rises above the eyebrow line. The possessor of Chess Ears is a strategist and, as the name implies, good at games of skill. He will rarely back away from a challenge and will never give up a struggle if there is the slightest chance that he can win. In life, as in games, he is enterprising and courageous. If Chess Ears are found in conjunction with a metal type of face then happy long-term relationships are foretold. However, the opposite is the case if found with a wood type of face. In either case, the happiest and most successful period of life is likely to be middle age.

The Water Ear

The water ear is set close to the head, is rather thick and soft with a large, well-rounded lobe. Like the metal ear, this type tends to rise above the eyebrow line and will tend to be lighter in colouration than the rest of the face. The water ear is the mark of someone who is very clever, quick-witted, intelligent and generally calm. It would take a lot of pressure to disturb the placid exterior of such a person so the possessor of this type of ear is bound to gain the reputation of being cool in a crisis. He will be a good negotiator, and will do well in business. However, strokes of misfortune and financial losses will be experienced if the water ear is found in conjunction with a Fire Face shape

The Chess Ear

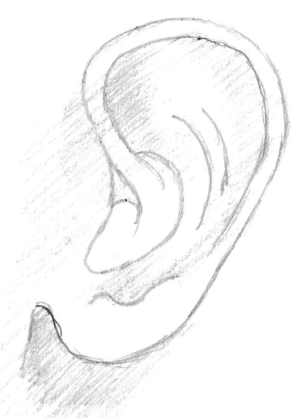

The Catching Wind Ear

The Touching Shoulder Ear

The ancient Chinese thought a lot of people with this feature. The Touching Shoulder Ear is also known as the Royal Ear and most descriptively as the Very Long Ear. Apart from the general length of the ear, it both rises above the eyebrow line, and reaches below the tip of the nose; the most noticeable feature of the ear is the ear pearl, which is thick, pendulous and rounded. This ear shape is connected with an authoritative manner. The possessor of such ears will rise high in life and achieve great things. He will also be wise and a capable advisor and administrator. He is capable of long periods of sustained effort to reach his ambitious goals. With such a person it would not be wise to imagine obstacles that he could not overcome.

The Catching Wind Ear

This sort of ear is wide and rounded with both the upper and middle wheels extending outwards from the head 'catching wind' so to speak. The possessor of Catching Wind Ears often had a rather upsetting childhood. There may have been an estrangement from the parents or at least an unsettled background. He may have left home early and so has known periods of isolation. Even so he has learned the benefits of hard work and ambition. Once he has set a goal this person will achieve it although he will need the comforting presence of a worthy and faithful partner to make him feel worthwhile.

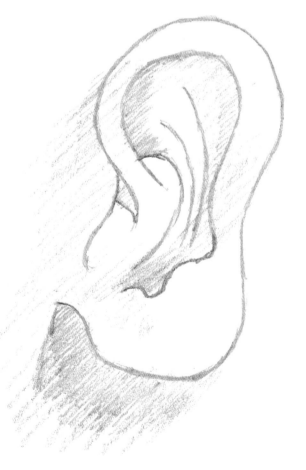

The Touching Shoulder Ear

The Upper Forward Ear

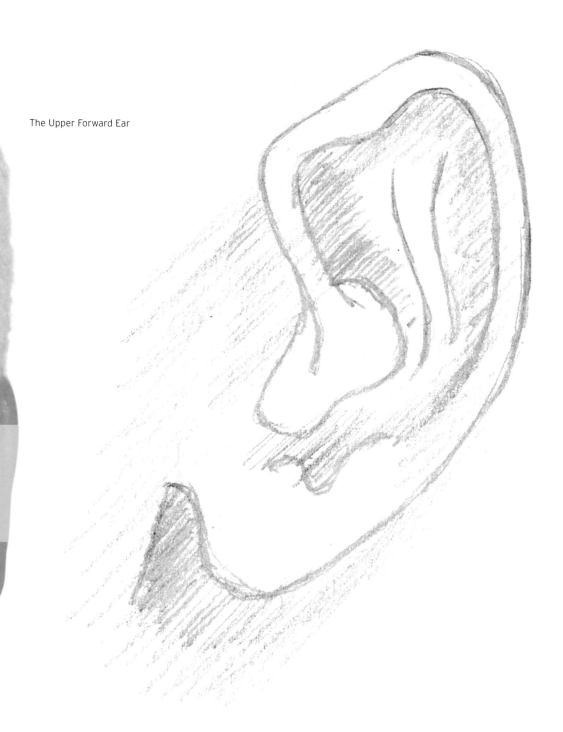

The Upper Forward Ear

The Upper Forward Ear is rather S shaped because the top of the ear slopes towards the eyebrow while sticking out somewhat, while the lobe tends to slope towards the back of the head. The lines of the inner and outer wheels melt into each other and are therefore indistinct. Ears like this are the mark of an extremely independent person who has a lot of pride and takes a long time to relate to others enough for him to trust them. He will prefer to sort out problems in solitude and generally refused to rely on anyone else. The Upper Forward Ear is also a sign that this person's life will have more than its fair share of ups and downs simply because his splendid isolation can cause as many problems as it cures.

The Pig Ear

This type of ear does not possess a distinct inner or outer wheel. In fact its shape is quite undefined almost being a sort of indistinct fleshy appendage on the side of the head. However it does tend to be rather thick and soft, in some ways it resembles the 'cauliflower ear' associated with ageing boxers. Aptly enough, this type of ear is associated with a hot and unruly temper. The possessor of this feature is easily goaded into rash actions and the inner frustrations will often boil over. It is also a mark of indecision and insecurity and many opportunities will be passed over simply because this person could not make up his mind in time. However, monetary good fortune is likely too, even though the possessor of the Pig Ear is neither careful nor wise with his cash.

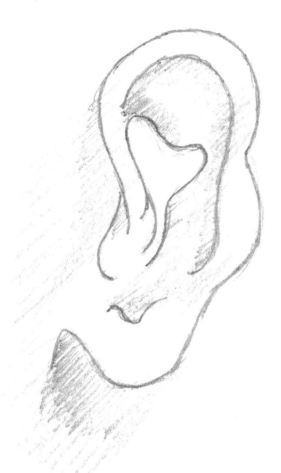

The Tiger Ear

The Tiger Ear

The Tiger Ear is small, hard and thick to the touch with an outer ring that is curled up tightly. The lines of the outer and inner wheels tend to melt into each other and are rather indistinct. These lines may also be broken or uneven. The Tiger Ear never sticks out; in fact one of the main give-away signs is that it clings tightly to the side of the head. The possessor of Tiger Ears is an honest person. He is straightforward and sometimes painfully forthright. Even so, his candour will win appreciation and admirers. He is decisive, has an impressive manner and qualities of leadership. Once this person has made a decision he sticks to it. A stranger to confusion, he prefers action to long drawn out analyses of future strategies.

The Pig Ear

The Rat Ear

The Rat Ear is small but full and rounded with a tightly curled outer wheel. The upper portion rarely rises above the eyebrow line. The unflattering description has very little to do with the dreaded rodent of the sewers. The ear is so called because the rat is the Chinese symbol of shrewdness, and possessors of this type of ear are certainly very astute. A person with Rat Ears will be extremely observant, and quick to take advantage of the slightest opportunity for profit. He will also be determined to get his own way, but he will not be hasty. In fact, his generally casual manner will mask a calculating mind. Be in no doubt, the actions of someone with Rat Ears is weighed up measured and planned out even if it seems he is being spontaneous.

The Rat Ear

The Porcupine Ear

The Porcupine Ear rises above the eyebrow line and the upper wheel is very wide. The rest of the ear is straight and hard to the touch. Traditionally, this type of ear is said to be 'strong in appearance'. The odd name ascribed to this type of ear is due to the nature of the porcupine in Chinese mysticism. This creature must be treated well or plagues and misfortunes will inevitably follow. Likewise the possessor of the Porcupine Ear demands respect and can be 'prickly'. He is an excellent judge of character and can be something of a cynic. However he has great vision and will win respect for his original turn of mind. He doesn't tend to be good with money and will find it difficult to settle down for any length of time

The Porcupine Ear

THE NOSE
AND CHEEKBONES

Before we can interpret the shape and configuration of the nose we have
to take into account the shape and positioning of the cheekbones.

The Cheekbones, The Guardsmen of the Face

One view of the ancient Chinese traditions of physiognomy holds that the nose is the emperor of the face. The cheekbones are thought to be like guardsmen or mandarins standing to attention on either side. Another viewpoint regards the nose as the 'fifth mountain', the central feature of the face which is like all other midpoints, middles and centres in oriental tradition, governed by the Earth element. The cheekbones themselves are the mountains of Wood and Metal respectively, the Wood being on the right and Metal on the left. The remaining two elements are facially represented by the forehead and the chin. The chin is the Fire mountain and the brow the Water mountain. Those who are familiar with Chinese astrology or with Feng Shui, the ancient art of placement, will already know that these elements are also represented by animal symbols. The Wood element (the left cheekbone in facial terms) is symbolised by the Green Dragon of the East. The right cheekbone, governed by the Metal element, is represented by the White Tiger of the West. The brow, under the rulership of the Fire element is symbolised as the Red Bird of the South,

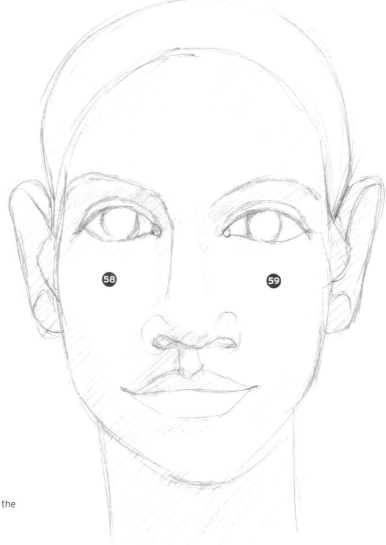

The age positions of the cheekbones

while the chin, governed by the Water element becomes the Black Tortoise of the North. This attribution of the symbolic creatures also provides the explanation for the description of the nose as the emperor of the face. This is because, the nose, being the central feature of the face belongs to Earth, one of that element's symbols being the Yellow Emperor.

In terms of the age positions, the cheekbones represent ages 58 on the right and 59 on the left.

The most important factors in determining the strength of weakness of the cheekbones is taking into account what they are not rather than what they are. In other words cheekbones are considered to support the nose therefore they should incline in the direction of the centre of the face. Flat or hollow cheekbones do not perform this function and the influence of the nose area is therefore weakened. So we are looking for possible factors that might change the role of the cheekbones.

If either of the cheekbones is noticeably higher than the other then the interpretation of the nose loses much of its importance. This is particularly the case if the left cheek is higher than the right. This factor increases a person's caution to the point of cowardice. A person with this feature is likely to do very little with his life simply because he does not dare.

If the nose is small and flat while the cheekbones protrude then it is said that 'the emperor is a puppet of his ministers'. A person with this feature is likely to be gullible and easily led.

Protruding cheekbones combined with very taut skin is an indication of bad luck. Opportunities may present themselves but circumstances will prevent a person with this feature from taking full advantage of them. He may find himself in the wrong place at the wrong time and to lose his gains as quickly as he received them. He may be a spendthrift with no thought for tomorrow.

Flat or dented cheekbones are indicative of shyness and possibly a lack of self-esteem. This sort of person avoids responsibility and prefers a quiet, uncomplicated life.

The six areas of the nose

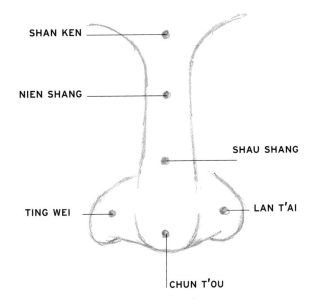

The Nose, The Emperor of the Face or Central Mountain

In general terms the nose should neither be too large or too small, too thin or too wide. The nostrils should not be too prominent and when one looks at a nose straight on it should not be possible to look up the nostrils. The skin of the nose should ideally be clear while the tip of the nose should be reasonably rounded and not too prominent.

The nose is divided into six distinct areas each known by a traditional Chinese name. The right nostril is called T'ing Wei while the left is known as Lan T'ai. The tip of the nose is Chun T'ou and the top of the nose as Shan Ken. Between them on the bridge of the nose lie the Nien Shang (at the end of the nose-bone) and Shou Shang (on the cartilage). These points are significant in terms of the age positions of the face. The Shan Ken relates to age 40, Nien Shang to 43, Shou Shang to 44 and Chun

T'ou at the tip to 47. The right nostril corresponds to age 48 while the left symbolises the 49th year.

Before we move on to the interpretation of individual nose profiles there are some overall points to be considered. As with all other forms of Chinese tradition a sense of proportion is important when it comes to examining the configuration of the nose. A long nose is considered to be preferable to a short one but this is only the case if it

does not overwhelm other features of the face.

A thin pointed nose is indicative of someone with an extremely independent nature. This person may be inwardly shy yet does not often show it. He may be ill at ease in company and have difficulty in revealing enough of his personality to make many friends. A noticeably

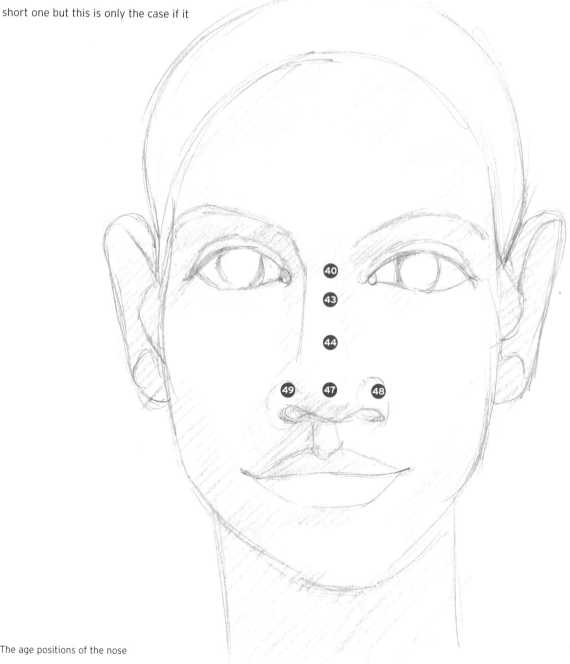

The age positions of the nose

large nose in combination with insignificant cheekbones is an indicator of recurring troubles within the family and reveals problematic relationships.

A very thin, beak-like nose placed high at the centre of the face is a sure indicator of a spendthrift nature. This is a lover of luxuries who can rarely afford his lifestyle.

A thin nose that starts high on the face with a noticeable (but not too prominent) nose-bone shows determination and an ability to make quick, correct decisions and stick to them.

If the bones that make up the structure of the nose are plainly visible then this is a person who will find it difficult to be corrected or to accept advice. While this

A very thin nose signifies and quick mind and swift perceptions. A person with this sort of nose will make fast decisions and stick to them

feature is a sign of wilfulness there is nevertheless a retiring nature and this person will withdraw rather than struggle against opposition.

A nose tip that is full and plump combined with wide nostrils is a sure indication of someone who has a very strong libido.

A soft, rounded nose is the mark of a person who has a sympathetic nature, is warm, loving and, to put it bluntly 'a soft touch'. Free with compassion, good advice and money, this type may be taken advantage of by 'hard nosed individuals'.

A thin nose that is reddish in colour suggests that its possessor is not at all good with cash. It is the mark of someone who is constantly in debt. If one nostril is higher than the other then a sharp, incisive nature is

A prominent, beak-like nose indicates a love of luxury and a spendthrift nature. A person with this type of nose often lives beyond his means

suggested. Shrewd, rather cunning and very perceptive, this type of person will be quick to make the most of any and all opportunities. He may also be lacking in conscience.

If there is a lump on either the Shou Shang or Nien Shang points then this person is likely to be eccentric and unpredictable. People around this individual will never know which way he will jump or what his reaction will be to their actions. This type of person has difficulty in relating to others and will experience many strained relationships due to communication problems.

If it is possible to look up the nostrils when the face is viewed straight on then this person will be extravagant with little understanding of the value of money. No sooner does cash arrive than it departs again... Usually to no good purpose. However if these forward-pointing nostrils happen to be thin and pinched there will also be a refusal to listen to advice, a complete conviction that

If the nostrils are lopsided then there is likely to be a lack of balance in life. This feature frequently denotes one who is as foolish as often as he is wise

their possessor always knows best and a forecast that his life will be filled with regrets.

Oval-shaped nostrils show that their possessor is very astute with his material resources and will prosper. There will be an essentially cautious, prudent nature and there will be a dislike of taking risks. Consequently, in times of trouble there will be ample resources to see him through.

Very rounded nostrils show a person who is an organiser by nature. He is a perfectionist who likes an orderly life, and that includes sorting out those around him too.

A pale nose, possibly with a grey tinge to the skin shows a person whose mind is constantly full of plans. New ideas are constantly being bounced around in his brain. This is not a person who gives in easily even when the odds against him seem insuperable. He instinctively knows that there is a solution to be found to the most intractable problem... If only he can work it out.

The fortunate possessor of oval-shaped nostrils will be very astute and do well financially. He will always have a back-up plan if ill fortune strikes

Nose Profiles

The Sword Nose

As the name implies this type of nose is long, sharp and pointed. It is generally bony and hard to the touch. The possessor of this type of nose is not the easiest person to get to know. He may seem aloof and unapproachable, yet underneath a natural reserve he is kindly. His relationship with his family will have often been tempestuous and there may be unresolved issues concerning his birth or early life. He may take his time in adapting to new situations but will generally be successful in life. The Emperor Napoleon Bonaparte possessed a splendid example of a sword nose.

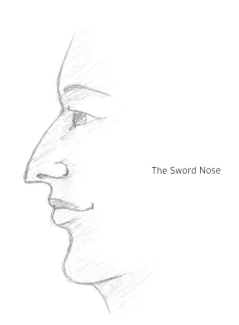

The Sword Nose

The Hairy Nose

The nostrils of this type of nose are particularly large, open and hairy. The body of the nose will be thick and strong, but the very tip will be rather thin and flat. The possessor of this nose is extremely competitive. Often experiencing luck in terms of the gaining of unearned money, he will nevertheless be quite spendthrift seeing life in terms of 'easy come, easy go'. This attitude will stand him in good stead when the going gets tough because he will not give in or succumb to despair. On the other hand, he will achieve success, not once but many times however he will find that such triumphs are fleeting and he will have to being again and again.

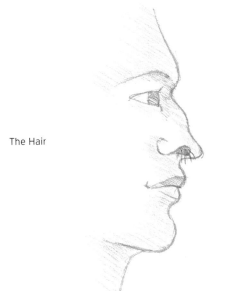

The Hair

The Lonely Mountain Nose

The tip of this type of nose will be high. The cheekbones and the middle portion of the nose (Nien Shang and Shou Shang) will be flat. The possessor of this nose will live a mainly contented life but circumstances will force him to settle for less than he would really like. His highest ambitions will be thwarted but nevertheless he will contrive a comfortable lifestyle and be generally happy with his companions. Hardships in early life convince him that the only true path is one of self-reliance. This is despite the fact that family and friends may wish to help him in times of difficulty. It may be that he is too proud to accept this assistance or that they are in no position to offer it.

The Lonely Mmountain Nose

The Bun-Bridge Nose

The bridge of this type of nose bulges outwards giving a mistaken impression of bulk, when actually the body of the nose is rather slim. The owner of this nose is good humoured and popular, generally getting on very well with people. However he does lack consistency and his behaviour will sometimes be extremely erratic. His life will be something of a roller coaster ride, having more than its fair share of high and low points. Friendships too may go through marked phases, different people fulfilling similar, necessary roles in this person's life at differing times. However, the Bun-bridge nose person is nothing if not courageous and above all, a survivor.

The Three-Bends Nose

The very top of the nose (the Shan Ken) will be deeply hollow, the bridge will bulge while the tip of the nose is sharp, thin and rather pointed. This type of nose is an indicator of mixed fortunes and sudden reversals of fate. Therefore at the lowest points in life unexpected opportunities and good fortune will suddenly occur. However, the reverse is also true, so that when he is at the top of the tree a branch is likely to break. However this type of personality is resilient and will learn how to handle these twists and turns in his fortunes. For this type of person life will be rarely, if ever boring.

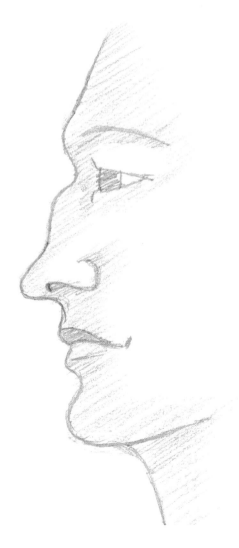

The Eagle Beak Nose

As the name implies, this type of nose resembles the beak of a bird of prey. It is hooked and sharp, curving outwards from the top. This is a person who relishes challenge. He rarely backs away from arguments or large projects. He is self-confident and quite formidable, always putting his own interests first. He could be intolerant and impatient with the inefficiencies or lack of purpose of others. He also tends to make his own luck because although opportunity will knock from time to time he has usually pre-empted the situation and has already made strides towards his goal.

The Collapsed Nose

The Collapsed Nose

The bridge of this type of nose will be dented or hollow. A nose that gently curves inwards from top to tip can be regarded as a form of Collapsed nose. A person with this feature is likely to be shrewd and rather self-serving. He is always on the lookout for an opportunity, a quick buck or the possibility of a wily manoeuvre. You can be sure that he in a winner even if his ideas are a little too high-flown for his own good. He may not make as much as he dreams of but even so he should do well materially speaking. He is also the type of person who loathes responsibilities and will go a long way to avoid trouble.

The Eagle Beak Nose

The Knot Nose

The Knot Nose can be of any shape, its defining feature being a protruding lump on the bridge of the nose, particularly situated on the Nien Shang. This is a feature belonging to a very strong willed person. He is someone who always thinks that he knows best in all circumstances. This individual would rather accept failure than act on the advice of another to avoid trouble. On the other hand, he is open handed with his resources, is possessed of a good and generous heart and win good friends and allies throughout life.

The Proturding Nostril Nose

The Protruding Nostril Nose

This nose is on the large side with a rounded, slightly upturned tip. From a straight on viewpoint it is possible to completely see both nostrils. This sort of person is easy going both with people and with money. When he is in funds he will spend freely and often dish out cash to all and sundry. Equally, when times are hard, he will not complain about his poverty. This type of character takes changes of fortune in his stride.

The Unbalanced Nostril Nose

The Unbalanced Nose

As the name suggests, one side of the nose is noticeably higher than the other. This is the mark of someone who will lose a great deal of money in his lifetime. Appointments will be missed and opportunities unwisely passed over. However, if the tip of the nose is rounded the interpretation is rather better, mitigating the losses and adding luck to an unfortunate fate. There will be no lack of initiative though and a great deal of wisdom can be gained because of troublesome life experiences.

The Philosopher's Son Nose

This type of nose has clear skin and is either straight or slightly curved. The Philosopher's Son Nose tends to be rather long, well balanced and somewhat pointed at the tip. The top of the nose is rather wide. The main impression of this kind of nose is aristocratic. Despite its appearance of nobility, the possessor of this nose is no snob. On the contrary, he is egalitarian and open-minded. He loves life and will treat everyone with equal respect. He will also possess a strong sense of right and wrong and will be ready to defend a point of principle to the hilt.

The Lamb Nose

The Lamb Nose is straight and quite strong for most of its length but the tip becomes rounded or even bulbous. The nostrils are clearly visible from the front. This is the mark of a hard-working individual who will achieve success by dint of unremitting effort. Noted for ambition, this type of individual is generally respected for his energy and determination. However he can harbour deep resentment if he is thwarted or obstructed. His relentless drive could possibly harm his personal relationships. Even so he is likely to be successful in his career.

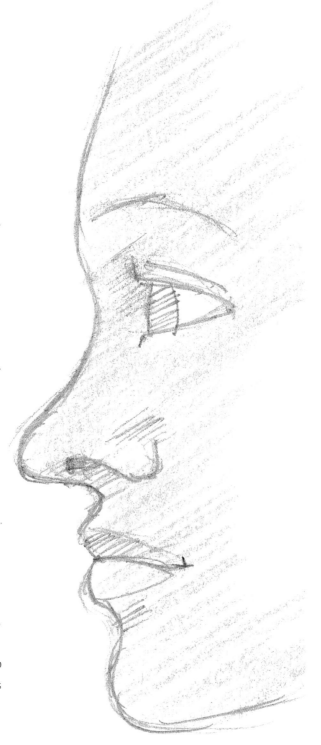

The Lamb Nose

The Deer Nose

This nose has the appearance of being rounded yet strong. The tip particularly is softened yet slightly protruding. The bridge of the nose may be curved inwards slightly. This nose indicates a kindly person who will keep his promises and be a support to those who need him. Fidelity is at the core of his character and he will stand by family, friends and colleagues through thick and thin. He also has an instinctive knack of surrounding himself with the right people. In addition the Deer-type nose is an indicator of longevity and probably of an extended family as well.

THE CHEEKLINES
OR FA LING

Many people possess a pair of creases that run downwards from the nose usually passing the Sea-Corners of the mouth. These are known as cheeklines or, by the ancient Chinese, Fa Ling. As usual, the shape and direction of the cheeklines can be interpreted according to the rules of face reading. In terms of the age positions of the face the Fa Ling relate to the mid-fifties. The left cheekline corresponds to the 55th year and the right cheekline to the 56th.

The age positions of the cheeklines

Parallel Fa Ling

If there are two parallel Fa Ling on either side of the mouth, or should there be a 'branch line' emerging from one of the cheeklines, this is a warning about financial stress. This person could have trouble keeping his gains and pressing circumstances will force him to squander his inheritance.

Mole Fa Ling

If there happens to be a dark mole or other protrusion on either of the Fa Ling then extravagance is likely to be a problem. The possessor of a mole in this region is not a saver and would far rather indulge his whims than invest for the future. He may also be constantly dissatisfied in his job. In some cases the presence of a blemish or mole on the Fa Ling can warn of danger in the 55th or 56th year. Abraham Lincoln had a protrusion on his right cheekline and was assassinated at the age of 56. However a red mark or mole on the tip of the tongue will neutralise this ominous prediction.

Parallel Fa Ling

Mole Fa Ling

Locking Fa Ling

Cheeklines that join the Sea-Corners of the mouth are said to be 'locking' and are not a desirable feature. The Chinese also refer to this feature as 'dragons entering the mouth'. Those with Locking Fa Ling are said to be prone to accidents and injury especially in middle age. However, some good news can be dredged from this circumstance because it is likely to be a life-transforming experience from which he will fully recover.

Crossed and Locking Fa Ling

If the cheeklines touch the corners of the mouth and are also crossed by creases descending from the cheeks, it is an indication of stomach ailments. A person with this feature should eat sensibly to avoid such problems as ulcers and food poisoning.

T'eng Snakes

In this case the Fa Ling curve inwards towards the corners of the mouth but do not end there. Before they touch the Ling, they again curve outwards and downwards towards the chin. This feature is the mark of someone who is generally carefree but can be extremely careless of both his own safety and his possessions.

Wide Fa Ling

Cheeklines that gently descend in a wide curve far out from the corners of the mouth are an indication of an innovative nature and of business success. This feature is also auspicious for those involved in creative and administrative fields.

Long, narrow Fa Ling

Fa Ling that descend sharply passed the corners of the mouth, possibly (but not necessarily) curving inwards below the bottom lip, are auspicious and denote a long life and robust health well into old age. However, if the cheeklines are particularly angular and pass the mouth in a straight line, their possessor is likely to be his own worst enemy, causing trouble with his words and unable to keep a promise.

Faint Fa Ling

An absence of cheeklines, or cheeklines that are indistinct or broken up into smaller lines, is indicative of luck. The possessor of this feature may not think of himself as particularly lucky because he often runs into troubled times. However, he would have to admit that he also tends to be rescued by the most unlikely circumstances. Having said that, this person is his own worst enemy, making bad decisions that will get him into trouble eventually.

Mandarin Fa Ling

Cheeklines of this type are usually deeply etched creases which are joined both by lines from the corners of the mouth and by lines rising upwards from the chin towards the cheeks. The reason that this feature is named after a high ranking official in the Chinese imperial court is that the possessor of this type of Fa Ling will rise to a prominent position and be capable of shouldering immense responsibilities. Such a one is destined for greatness.

Unequal or Meandering Cheeklines

Fa Ling of unequal lengths or cheeklines that follow a different path to each other indicate that the possessor of this feature lacks persistence and may be unstable. Such a person is likely to suffer great disappointments especially in his mid-fifties.

Upward Curving Cheeklines

If the Fa Ling have a marked upward curve in the direction of the cheekbones the outlook is not good. In fact tradition states that the possessor of such cheeklines will know much tragedy and may suffer illness and misfortune.

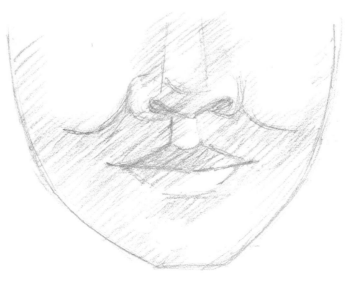

THE LIPS AND MOUTH

The shape and relative size of the mouth can tell a lot about an individual's
character and fortune. Along with the eyebrows this facial feature is an
indicator of mood, showing happiness or misery, generosity or meanness, often
in swift succession. Likewise, the conformation of the mouth and lips are said
to show the habitual traits that have developed throughout life.

According to the rules of the age positions of the face the upper lip corresponds to the early fifties namely ages 51 (on the right) and 52 (on the left), while the lower lip has 53 (on the right) and 54 (on the left). The middle of the lower lip connects to the end of that decade symbolising the 59th year.

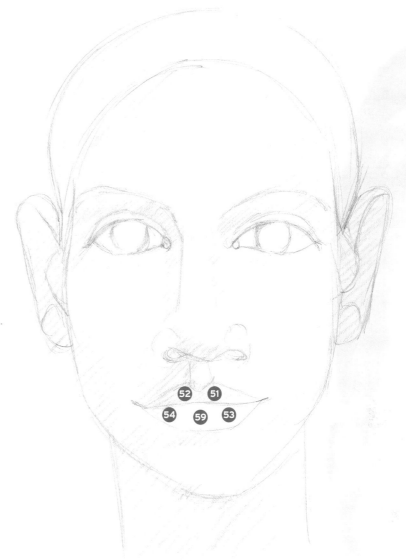

The Perfect Lips

In the most ideal case the lips should be full and fairly prominent and in proportion to the size of the face as a whole, being neither too small and pinched, nor too extravagantly large. Having said that, tradition states that it is better to have a large mouth set in a small face than the opposite because a small mouth tends to detract from a person's luck.

The proportions of the lips, and indeed the mouth as a whole should be moderate and of equal size with both the upper and lower portions, even and of a light red colouration. This denotes a character that is stable and honest

Each half of the mouth should be the mirror image of the other and should be able to close without leaving a gap between them. The lips should also have a 'natural radiance', in other words they should be lightly moistened. In the case of a man, the lips should be firm but not too hard, while in the case of a woman they should be soft but not flabby.

Should you be fortunate enough to possess such a 'perfect' mouth then the ancient art of face reading proclaims that you will be warm, loving, charitable, honest, resolute and respected. It also goes on to state that the greatest success in life will be started in your fourth decade and continue to great acclaim after your fiftieth year.

The age positions of the upper lip relate to the 51st and 52nd years. The lower lip relates to ages 53, 54 and 59

The extremely lucky possessor of perfect lips will be loving, charitable and respected. He will achieve great acclaim after his 50th year

Sea-Corners or Ling which rise from the mouth's edges reflect a refined character who has a love of culture and artistic ability

The Sea-Corners of the Mouth

The corners of the mouth are called 'Ling' or Sea-Corners and these should be slightly turned upwards to denote a happy personality. It also indicates a creative nature with artistic talent and an appreciation of culture. If, however the ling are inclined downwards the indications are of materialistic attitudes and a more practical, down to earth frame of mind. It can also indicate inner anxieties about personal security.

The Large Mouth

A wide mouth with full lips is said to be more fortunate than having a small one even though it does lend itself to exaggeration and boasting. It is also the mark of someone who is popular, outgoing and the life and soul of any gathering. However the possessor of this feature may lack any clear purpose in life and rarely carry any of his plans through to a successful conclusion. Perhaps because if his undoubted popularity, he may consort with 'bad company' and earn the disapproval of his family. This is likely to be the case especially with men with large mouths, however women with this feature can do somewhat better because they tend to do well in business and may find remarkable success in the entertainment industries.

A large mouth with weak, uneven Sea-Corners and unequal lips is indicative of someone who acts before he thinks, and always blames others for his own mistakes. It can show bitterness and a sharp tongue. This is a person who lives in constant danger of financial loss through his own intemperate words and actions.

If the full lips are bright and well-balanced tradition states that this is a sign of robust good health and a strong stomach (the Chinese credit the stomach with

A large mouth is said to be better than a small one even though it does show a character given to exaggeration and boasting

great importance, some actually think it is the seat of reason, the process of digestion being analogous to thought). The possessor of these large lips will enjoy all that life has to offer although he may be somewhat greedy.

Although this is not strictly part of Chinese face reading, certain traditions hold that if a person with a stocky body shape also possesses a large mouth one can deduce that he is extremely determined. He will not allow difficulties to obstruct his path or to be easily deterred from a course of action. He may not always be successful but this does not worry him because there are always more challenges to be found. He cannot be said to be the most self aware of individuals because his busy life leaves little time for reflection or regret.

The Small Mouth

People with small mouths often lack confidence and are constantly seeking the approval of others. It may also point to suspicious attitudes and close attention to other people's motives. Caution is the natural watchword of this type, and this trait is often applied to their finances. Meanness is likely to be a major characteristic if the lips are also thin. Thin lips may indicate that this is a person with very few close relationships, one who will live a lonely life in middle age.

A small, pinched mouth indicates a lack of self confidence and may point to suspicious attitudes and meanness

The Meeting of the Lips

The Straight Line Meeting

The way that the upper and lower lips meet is of great importance in Chinese face reading. Those that meet in a straight line show someone who is logical, orderly and fairly unemotional. Indeed there may be a singular lack of emotional responses in this person, sometimes to the detriment of the relationships.

The Straight Line Meeting suggests someone who tends to be unemotional, logical and orderly in his approach to life

The Downward Central Kink

Lips that have a downward pointing deviation in the middle of lips that are otherwise straight suggest a character that is outwardly conventional, stable and perfectly normal in the context of society. However there is a boiling passion concealed beneath the placid exterior.

An individual with a Downward Central Kink may possess an conventional, placid exterior that belies his passionate interior

Pursed Lips

Lips that become naturally pursed together when the mouth is closed show a great deal of worry. It may also point to a frustrated and bad tempered individual who tries far too hard to please those in authority.

The Gently Curved Meeting

Those lips that meet in a gently curve that turns up slightly at the Sea-Corners reveal a personality that is friendly and open yet is capable of self-assertion. If the lips are also full then he will be a competent organiser of others and will probably be found in a responsible position. If these lips are particularly thick and red then a sensuous nature is revealed as well as the possibility of numerous risky love affairs.

The Gently Curved Meeting

The Open Meeting

Lips that do not quite close when the mouth is closed leaving a small gap usually at the centre of the mouth are indicative of wit. However, it can also show misfortunes, particularly in the early years of the fifth decade (this is the time span that is traditionally governed by this area of the face see pp.18-20). As a point of interest, the great philosopher Confucius (Kung Fu Tse) possessed this feature as well as buck teeth (see The Fire Blowing Mouth p.110).

The Upwardly Curving Uneven Meeting

Lips whose course is wavering and slightly upwardly curving indicate a character who is eloquent, persuasive and creative. However, they do tend to have a scheming side and often conceal their true motives from others. This is especially true when it comes to their sexual nature, where their powers of creating plausible word pictures makes them both charming seducers and cunning concealers of the truth.

The Very Uneven Meeting

The Very Uneven Meeting

If the lips are the mirror image of each other and meet in a very uneven line full of small deviations from the straight, it denotes a personality who is likewise filled with deviations from the straight and narrow. This feature can show a deeply troubled individual who feels misunderstood and isolated. Although the sexual nature is strong, and success in this field almost guaranteed, lasting relationships tend to elude him. Full sensuous lips that meet in this way further serve to emphasise the power of the libido. This trait will almost inevitably lead to unwise encounters with major repercussions.

Traditional Mouth Shapes

As usual in Chinese face reading there are certain mouth shapes which have earned symbolic if sometimes unflattering names.

The Square Mouth

This traditional mouth shape is defined by thick red lips that appear to be rather angular and squarish. This type of mouth is considered to be very fortunate and denotes happiness and success both in the public and private spheres of life. It also shows honesty, stability and the respect of others.

The Creative Mouth

This mouth shape is slightly upturned giving the Sea-Corners a smiling appearance, possibly with a defining crease around them. The lips are thick, red, moist and well shaped. This is the mouth of someone who is artistically talented, clever and forthright. The candour of his opinions will be sought and appreciated by his many friends. He is a person of good humour and generosity.

The New Moon Mouth

As the name describes, the mouth is shaped very much like a new moon with the Sea-Corners inclined into a permanent smile. This is a person with a logical mind, one who can argue his point eloquently and with considerable force and persuasion. This person has the ability to concentrate deeply and is extremely tenacious. The possessor of the New Moon Mouth is also likely to be artistically gifted.

The Fire Blowing Mouth

This type of mouth has down-turned corners and pursed lips. The upper lip has a sharp downward deviation in the middle. The lips of this type of mouth tend to be rather thin and the upper front teeth may protrude slightly. The ancient Chinese thought of this shape as resembling the mouth of an acrobat or entertainer blowing flame as a part of his act. This is a feature possessed by a loner, an individualist. He may find it difficult to establish lasting friendships and will find common ground with few. Events in early life may have left a painful emotional mark and he often feels resentful or rejected. However he will eventually find soul mates who will bolster his confidence and with whom he can be happy.

The Dry, Uneven Mouth

The lips of this type of mouth tend to be rather dry and dull in colour. The Sea-Corners slope sharply downwards and the whole appearance of the mouth is irregular. This is the feature of someone who is quite unique. In fact he may find it hard to find a role in life or a career which really suits him. Financial problems will be a recurring pattern throughout life, but he has patience and determination enough to get through them. Trust is an issue with this person and it will take great persistence to get to know him well.

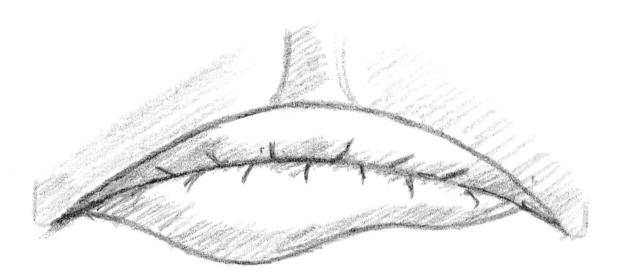

The Fish Mouth

The Ling or Sea-Corners of this type of mouth slope sharply downwards to noticeable points, in addition, the lips of the Fish Mouth tend to be thin. This is mouth of a person who has been forced to rely on the help and financial support of his family. Possibly due to an unconventional career choice or, possibly due to an extended period spent in higher education. Indeed this person will have difficulty in finding a suitable life path. However once this is found, then success will follow.

The Lotus Leaf Mouth

The lips of the Lotus Leaf are thin with dull colouration. This type of mouth is particularly long and slightly down-curved. It is the feature possessed by someone who is very private and finds it almost impossible to talk about his own affairs, his weaknesses or to admit to his faults. This is because he rarely admits such things to himself. Consequently he will find it galling to accept criticism. On the whole, he is far more comfortable discussing abstract matters or gossiping about other people's foibles.

The Unbalanced Mouth

The general appearance of this type of mouth is lopsided. One of the Sea-Corners inclines downwards while the other slopes up. The possessor of this feature is a real talker who is an entertaining companion. He is somewhat inclined to exaggerate but that is often done only for dramatic effect. When dealing with this person it is important to remember that he is very sensitive and uses the constant barrage of repartee as a cover for his insecurities. He will be lucky with money but also inclined to spend more than can be afforded.

The Cherry Mouth

The Cherry Mouth is considered to the most auspicious of all the traditional types. It is rounded with upward sloping corners. The lips are full and red, while the teeth are small, white and close together (teeth of this type are called 'pomegranate teeth'). This type of mouth is a feature possessed by a person who is wise beyond his years. He is also likely to be intelligent and insightful. It would not be unusual for this person to be dishing out sage advice almost constantly. Many people will have cause to be grateful to him and he will, eventually have many influential friends who will be willing to help him if ever he is in need.

The Smile

The way that someone smiles is a revealing indicator of character and attitudes towards you. Bearing this in mind the ancient Chinese sages devised a set of simple rules to be used in conjunction with the overall interpretation of the mouth and lips.

The first and foremost of these is never trust someone who smiles without revealing their teeth. Such a person has something to hide and this secret is probably to your detriment.

If the smile reveals the upper teeth but not the gums, it is a sure sign of a generous spirit, an open nature and an auspicious fate. When both the upper and lower teeth are visible in the smile this interpretation is doubled, although such a gift for popularity will win this person envious enemies too (it is claimed that women of loose virtue often possess such smiles). If the smile also shows the upper gums then this person is likely to be prone to depression.

The Tongue

Although the tongue is not strictly speaking part of the face, it nevertheless does have some traditional meanings according to this ancient oriental art. The ideal tongue should be large and wide, moving quickly when one speaks. The outlook is even better if the tongue is deep red because this will bestow honour and respectability.

Short tongues are not considered to be auspicious. Long tongues are very lucky, especially if the person possessing one can touch the end of his nose with the tip of his tongue. This peculiar ability is said to bestow long life, prosperity and remarkable luck. However if the tongue is particularly long and narrow there will be unexpected reversals of fortune and disappointments. A tongue that is short and rough also shares this gloomy outlook.

A person's smile is very revealing of character and attitudes towards you. Make sure that you note whether the gums are visible when a person smiles in your direction

If there happen to be wrinkles running the length of the tongue then the possessor of this feature will be honest and trustworthy. However, cross-wise wrinkles on the tongue are the mark of short temper and hasty words. If both lengthwise and crosswise wrinkles are present then this can be an indication of an outstanding career and financial good fortune.

THE PHILTRUM
OR JEN CHUNG

The philtrum is the groove that connects the nose to the centre of the upper lip. It has a unique importance in the art of face reading because it not only reveals how fertile a person is likely to be but also has a bearing on his prospects of longevity.

In Chinese tradition the philtrum is known as Jen Chung or the 'middle man'. Just as the cheekbones can be thought of as guardsmen, the Jen Chung can be symbolised as a minister or messenger of the emperor. In fact, this groove can be thought of as a channel directing the energies of the Emperor of the face (the nose) to the mouth. This area of the face is also symbolic of the fiftieth year of life.

In men, the appearance of hair within the philtrum is considered to be a good omen because this feature denotes an ability to make friends easily and to become popular. The opposite is the case when no hair is found within the Jen Chung because such a person will easily offend others and make unnecessary enemies. A man with a bald philtrum will find that his fifth decade is likely to be troubled by incessant quarrels.

The age position of the philtrum

The Long, Deep Philtrum

This is the best type of philtrum to possess. It is notable because it is long, straight, deep and broad. Fertility is emphasised by such a feature and it is a sure indication of good fortune and long life. The fiftieth year will also see remarkable advances in this person's status, to such an extent that it is likely that the events of the whole decade will be favourable.

The Narrow-Based Philtrum

When the Jen Chung is wider at the top and rather narrow in the area just above the upper lip 'the messages of the Emperor are lost'. In other words, there is a constriction of energy that can indicate failing health and low fertility. It is therefore unlikely that the possessor of this feature will have many children, mostly daughters.

The Shallow Philtrum

Possessing a Jen Chung which is shallow almost to the point of flatness is not a good sign. Traditional interpretations of this feature suggest that good fortune tends to elude is possessor. It also suggests a person of slender means and few if any children.

The Narrow-Based Philtrum

The Wide-Based Philtrum

A Jen Chung that is wider at the base than at the top is usually an indication of many descendants. The possessor of this feature is likely to be the parent of an extensive brood. Some sources suggest that offspring are likely to be born in later life. It is also suggested that this person will have more sons than daughters.

The Wide-Based Philtrum

The Wide Mid-Point Philtrum

A philtrum whose widest point is in its midsection is not considered as an active channel but rather as a still lake. This generally indicates a period of stagnation in one's affairs around the age of fifty. It may also suggest a period of illness, depression or loss around this time.

The Short Philtrum

If the gap between nose and lip is noticeably small, the philtrum will likewise be short. Although this feature is not conducive to longevity it nevertheless points to a life that is lived to the full with some remarkable achievements contained within it. Alexander the Great, who conquered the known world, had a very short philtrum and had ended his career before his thirty-third birthday.

The Fading Philtrum

If the Jen Chung descends from the nose and then fades completely before it reaches the upper lip it is considered to be a misfortune. Traditional authorities state that this feature can be an indication of early death or at least of severe loss and illness. If, however, the philtrum is itself long then the fact that it fades becomes less important. However, the declining years will be troubled by the disputes of one's children. A sense of isolation would also figure in the interpretation of this fairly rare feature.

The Bent Philtrum

If the philtrum noticeably inclines to either the right or the left its asymmetry will affect the balance of the whole face. This is not considered to be a good omen and suggests frustrated purpose and failure. The possessor of this feature may lose his direction in life, become depressed and suffer financial hardship. A bent philtrum also suggests childlessness.

The Creased Philtrum

Creases or wrinkles on the Jen Chung, whether they are vertical or horizontal are considered to be bad signs. If the wrinkles are horizontal, family and business anxieties will afflict your fiftieth year, and possibly ruin the chances of a contented middle age. The outlook is somewhat better if the creases are vertical, running upwards from the lip towards the nose. In this case the conception of children will occur later in life. Chinese authorities are quite specific about the ages that the offspring will arrive. According to them a man will become a father in his fifties, while a woman with this feature will first conceive when she is forty. For both men and women this will be a worrying time.

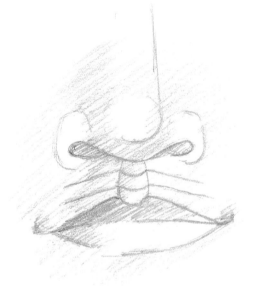

The chin is also described as the Mountain of the Black Tortoise, and its very shape is reminiscent of a turtle's shell. It is the fifth of the 'five mountains' of the face, the others being the nose, the forehead and the two cheekbones.

THE CHIN AND JAW

The chin is considered to be the foremost indicator of willpower in the art of Kang Xiang. We all instinctively know the difference between a weak and strong chin, and indeed our received knowledge on the subject is totally in tune with the interpretation according to Chinese face reading. It is also indicative of how susceptible we are to giving in to temptations of one sort or another. Since this area is associated with the early sixties to early seventies it can also indicate the capacity to retain or lose wealth in old age. The fleshy area just below the mouth corresponds to the sixties while the points along the lower part of the jawline represent the seventies.

The ideal chin should be quite broad and full, but not so prominent that it becomes the most noticeable feature of the face. And, just as the chin is the foremost point of the lower jaw, its shape will be reflected in the jawbone itself. Thus a narrow jaw will invariably accompany a narrow, pointed chin, while a wide, rectangular chin will have a broad jaw line. These features, more than any other, have an influence on the general face shape (see pp.8–15).

As with most other individual features in face reading, there are different types of chin, each of which has its own interpretation. It is important to remember that the broader the chin happens to be the more strength and determination is added to the character.

The age position of the chin and jaw

The Rounded Chin

This type of chin is associated with emotional warmth and openhearted generosity. It also signifies a certain personal ease and the ability to make the best of any situation. A person possessing this sort of chin will make himself at home in any company and adapt his responses to his surroundings. If this sort of chin also happens to be short, all the above characteristics are emphasised while adding charm to the personal make-up. A rounded chin that is longer and more prominent usually indicates someone who can use his charm to good advantage, winning people to his side and easily out-manoeuvring rivals. This type of person would make an excellent populist politician.

The Square Chin

A square-cut chin is associated with hard work, high achievement and considerable self-will. The square chin is often cited as a desirable feature in the clean-cut American boy. Be that as it may, this type of chin denotes a character that is trustworthy and steadfast, honourable in all type of partnerships, both emotional and business and above board in all his dealings. The feelings run very deep in this type of person, but he may lack charm. He is definitely a 'take him as you find him' sort of person. A dimple or vertical cleft on this type of chin is an endearing feature showing the possibility of youthful rejection and a subsequent need to be loved. This cleft or groove is often found in artists and performers the most notable of whom is the Hollywood great, Kirk Douglas.

The Broad Jutting Chin

Similar in appearance and interpretation to the Square Chin (above), this type tends to protrude somewhat adding to the inner strength and honourable intentions of its possessor. However, the owner of this type of chin is often more 'pushy' and demanding than is someone with the square kind. He may also be an incorrigible seducer, undeniably attractive but unable to restrain his mating urge. This feature does not make the owner of the broad, jutting chin a faithful spouse even though his magnetism and personal charisma will be very strong indeed. A good example of a person with a broad, jutting chin was the late American President John F. Kennedy. He was a person whose many fine qualities did not extend to fidelity to his wife Jackie.

The Narrow or Pointed Chin

A chin that is narrow or pointed is one of the types often described as being weak, and has a far less attractive interpretation than the kinds previously mentioned. The willpower of the owner of the narrow or pointed chin is indeed far weaker and there may be periods of depression that sap his energies and undermine his plans. This type of chin is also a bad omen for old age because it foretells of many troubles, family disputes and loneliness. In the case of a chin that is very pointed, the Ancient Chinese flatly state that the outlook is bleak and may even presage an early demise.

The Receding Chin

If it is possible, the interpretation of the receding chin is even worse than that of the narrow variety. The unfortunate possessor of this type of chin will be assailed by negativity of every type. It tells of a character low in self -esteem, indecisive, uncertain and prone to ill health. If the receding chin is narrow the interpretation remains the same, no better nor worse. However, if the chin also happens to be broad an obstinate trait is also added. This means that although this person will still find it difficult to reach decisions, once he has done so he will stick to them through thick and thin, even when they are proven to be wrong. The personality flaws foretold by the receding chin have an equally unfortunate outcome leading to an old age made irksome by solitude, poverty and bitterness.

The Beard

The pattern of a man's hair growth in the region of the chin and jaw can give another level of interpretation to this region of the face. When assessing this factor, the colour, density and direction of the growth are important. In general hair growth only occurs around the areas of the philtrum or Jen Chung (pp.114-118), the chin and along the jaw line and above. Of course these regions have individual ages associated with them ranging from the early fifties to the middle nineties and it is with these periods of life that the interpretation of the beard is concerned.

The Ideal Beard

The best and most fortunate type of beard to possess is one whose hairs are dark in hue. The hair should be fine, soft to the touch and shiny. It should not close in around the mouth too much but should reveal some skin both above and below the lips. This type of beard reveals an honest and thrifty nature, hard working and generous. It also foretells that the late middle and old age will be vigorous, happy and blessed with good health.

A beard with hair that is fine, soft and shiny is considered to be ideal, revealing an honest and thrifty nature

The Coarse Beard

If the hair growth is of thick, wiry, dull hair that is rough to the touch it can undo the interpretation of the chin itself. A beard such as this denotes a mean streak and boorish behaviour. The owner of this type of beard is likely to be quarrelsome, ill tempered and easily provoked. If this unfortunate interpretation is worsened by hair growth very near to the mouth then there is also the threat of violent injury during middle age.

The Patchy Beard

A thin growth of hair or a beard that is patchy in appearance is an indicator of a weak, indecisive character. In many ways this is a hirsute equivalent of the receding chin, although its meaning is not quite so bad. However it can show many periods of ill health especially as this person's age increases. If this patchy growth is accompanied by a bald philtrum then misfortunes will be complicated by unjust slander and adverse criticism.

A thin, patchy beard made up of wiry hair is indicative of a weak, indecisive character and the possibility of unjust slander

Index

Bibliography & Acknowledgements

The World Atlas of Divination,
John Matthews, Headline, 1982

The Way to Chinese Astrology,
Jean-Michel Huon de Kermadec,
Unwin Paperbacks, 1986

How to Read Faces,
Rodney Davies, Aquarian Press, 1989

Body Reading,
Sasha Fenton, Aquarian Press, 1990

Chinese Animal Symbolisms,
Ong Hean-Tatt, Pelanduk Publications, 1993

The New Chinese Astrology,
Suzanne White, Pan, 1994

Chinese Face and Hand Reading,
Man-Ho Kwok, Piatkus, 1995

Chinese Divinations,
Sasha Fenton, Zambezi , 2001

Feng Shui From Scratch,
Jonathan Dee, D&S Books, 2001

Picture Credits

Face and feature illustrations by Peter Mallison.
Illustrations pp26–27 by Pauline Cherrett.
Photographs pp 2, 6, 7, 31, 113 © Stockbyte.
Jacket (and page border) face model – Ray Pawlett.

Dedication

To Grant.
And with special thanks to Sasha and Jan.